C000244195

On the
SOMME

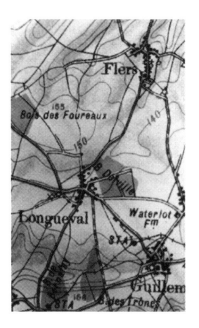

The Kitchener Battalions
of the Royal Berkshire Regiment

1916

Colin Fox

John Chapman   Martin McIntyre

Ian Cull   Len Webb

Cover illustration

Illustrated on the cover is the cap badge of the Royal Berkshire
Regiment. The China Dragon emblem is a reminder that a
forerunner of the Regiment, the 49th Regiment of Foot, fought
in the the Opium Wars in China from 1839 to 1842.

(Amalgations in 1959 and 1994 led to the formation of the
new Royal Gloucestershire, Berkshire and Wiltshire Regiment).

Photographs which accompany the text are taken from family
papers, authors' collections and *Berkshire and the War* (by kind
permission of the Reading Evening Post). Individual acknowl-
edgment is given of those photographs reproduced by kind
permission of the Imperial War Museum and the Public
Record Office.

Designed by Jonathan Nock (student) and printed in
the Department of Typography & Graphic Communication,
The University of Reading

ISBN 0 7049 1160 4

1996

Foreword

I am greatly privileged to write the Foreword for this second
booklet in the series 'Responding to the Call', produced by the
research team at the University of Reading under the guidance
of Colin Fox and telling us about the Battle of the Somme in
1916.

The team is to be congratulated and thanked for presenting
such a comprehensive, detailed and absorbing picture of life at
the Front in that year as experienced by so many Royal Berkshiremen and their compatriots in the Great War.

One of the main aims of the research, as stated, is to build up
a resource base for family and local historians. This booklet
uniquely covers the demoralising experiences of officers and
men in the three Royal Berkshire 'Service' Battalions at the
Battle of the Somme in 1916. As such this modest aim is more
than successfully attained but, perhaps more importantly, the
authors present a story of great national value, not only for the
events themselves but also as an example of dogged British ded-
ication to a cause by the rank and file of a proud County
Regiment often under extreme conditions of warfare. The picture that emerges is of endurance, bravery and exceptional
resilience by the officers and men, many with no more than one
year's military training.

The Royal Berkshire volunteers of Kitchener's Army proved, in
the end, that they could outlast and defeat their highly trained
German enemy by doing their 'duty' in the trenches and in 'No
Man's Land' at the River Somme – day after day and night after
night.

The scale of human slaughter and suffering was appalling by
any standards. Overall, a total of 19 Divisions took part in all
the Somme battles. On the first day – 1 July 1916 – over 50,000
casualties was the price paid, '…we, the assailants were mowed
down in swathes…'. The Official History of the war bleakly
states: 'To have reached the German trenches at all was an outstanding feat of arms.' So it continued through 1916 with all
three battalions rotating between front and rear areas in the

battle arena subjected to shelling even when out of the front line. The term 'poor bloody infantry' was not acquired without good reason.

This booklet describes how the 5th, 6th, and 8th Battalions of the Royal Berkshire Regiment played their part, narrated through the eyes of the officers and men who had answered Kitchener's call for volunteers and who survived to tell the tale. Civilians from all walks of life. How proud Lord Kitchener would have been had he lived to see their spirit and determination at the Somme battles; unfortunately he met an untimely death by drowning when his ship was mined on 6 June 1916.

At the Somme, Haig, the British C-in-C, aimed at creating a breach in the formidable German defence system through which cavalry would burst. Manoeuvre warfare would then create the conditions for victory. (A useful appendix is included for those wishing to visit the Somme battlefields to relive this epic story).

In the event, the Somme battles of 1916 made only limited gains and cost some 400,000 casualties, demonstrating the brutality and ineffectiveness of frontal attacks against formidable trench systems, covered by artillery, mines and wire.

On 1 July, tanks had not yet made their appearance on the battlefield and air support took the form of artillery spotting and reconnaissance. Only 28 aircraft were available for interdiction tasks on rear areas and none for close support bombardment of enemy positions. Lessons were learned and improvements made as the battle progressed.

In today's technological world, the primitive communication system is also of note. Long distance information on the battlefield relied on carrier pigeons carried by signallers with forward units. Field Marshal Bernard Montgomery – a Brigade Major on the Somme in 1916 – describes in his memoirs how a pigeon, expected from the front with vital information for the brigade commander, arrived with a message strapped to its leg sent by its frustrated handler. It read: 'I am absolutely fed up with carrying this bloody bird about France!' Monty also highlights in his memoirs the absence of contact by higher commanders and staff officers with the troops at the sharp end: 'I never once saw the British Commander-in-Chief, neither French nor Haig and only twice did I see any Army Commander.'

The antagonism between the staff, safely installed in rear areas, and the forward troops was, at best, summed up by a music hall joke: 'If bread be the staff of life, what is the life of the Staff? – one big loaf!' Of such were the feelings in 1916 when, as the mini-biographies and reminiscences of the survivors disclose, the infantry, for the most part, were enmeshed in their trenches or clawing their way over the parapets in chaotic conditions through mines and barbed wire defences. Artillery barrages and machine guns enfiladed along the German trench systems made them, quite simply, cannon fodder.

It is against this background that these wartime civilian volunteer service battalions gave of their all. As the story illustrates, few indeed returned and as Cole and Priestley's *Outline of British Military History* (1936) states: 'No other army in the whole history of war ever previously attacked positions so naturally strong and so carefully prepared.'

This impeccably researched account of how our forebears in the 5th, 6th and 8th Battalions of the Royal Berkshire Regiment acquitted themselves, not only provides invaluable historical background on a national scale but also gives pride and encouragement to a very wide readership; in particular to their relatives and to the Regiment's successors in today's army – the officers and men of the Royal Gloucestershire, Berkshire and Wiltshire Regiment.

The battle honour 'Somme 1916' gained for the Regiment will be remembered as an example and symbol of duty done for monarch and country by these three gallant battalions striving against all odds and decimated while responding to 'The Call'.

John Hill (Colonel, retired)
The Royal Berkshire Regiment
1938–1961

Acknowledgements

We should like to acknowledge the many generous
acts of support which have made this booklet possible.

Our thanks go to:
    Mr Alan Ault
    Mr Henry Gold
    Wg Cmdr TFH Hudson (rtd)
    Mr EF Malet de Carteret
    Mrs Celia Mosley
    Mr Andrew Tatham
    Mr PA Watkins
for giving us access to private papers.

Thanks for helpful guidance go to the staffs of the following
institutions:
    Berkshire County Reference Library, Reading
    Commonwealth War Graves Commission, Maidenhead
    Imperial War Museum, London
    Newbury Public Library
    Public Record Office, Kew
    Royal Gloucestershire, Berkshire and Wiltshire Regiment
    (Salisbury) Museum
        whose curator, Major JH Peters MBE, has taken a sympa-
        thetic interest in our work from the very beginning.

We are grateful to colleagues:
    Paul Reed, our man on the Somme, gave us the benefit
    of his unrivalled knowledge of the battlefield.

    Dr Julia Boorman and Dr Barry Croucher read drafts of the
    material and gave us useful critical comments. Any errors,
    omissions or infelicities which may remain are however our
    responsibility.

    To Jonathan Nock and the Department of Typography &
    Graphic Communication at The University of Reading we
    are indebted for the design, typesetting and printing of
    the booklet.

Preface

This is the second of a series of booklets which are designed to commemorate and document the participation of three battalions of the Royal Berkshire Regiment in the Great War. The three – the 5th, 6th and 8th – were all New Army or 'Kitchener' battalions, recruited by voluntary enlistment after the outbreak of war, and they all saw service on the Western Front between 1915 and 1918.

The first booklet, 'Responding to the Call', was published in 1995 and traced the fortunes of two of the battalions – the 5th and the 8th – during their first major engagement with the German army at the Battle of Loos in September and October 1915.

This volume appears in the 80th anniversary year of the Battle of the Somme and covers the experiences of all three battalions in 1916. Pride of place is given to the 6th Battalion because this was their first major action and they were present throughout the campaign. The aim here, as with 'Responding to the Call', is to present a narrative of events supported and amplified by personal testimony.

The research project out of which these publications arose was initiated as part of the Extramural Studies programme of the University of Reading. The project had as one of its aims the creation of a resource base on individual members of the battalions which might be of use to family and local historians. In fulfilment of this aim a database has been created and made available on computer at the Royal Gloucestershire, Berkshire and Wiltshire Regiment (Salisbury) Museum.

The research team is continuing its work and hopes to publish further booklets covering the years 1917 and 1918. The team would be interested to hear from anyone who has information about members of the three battalions, especially in the later period of the war. Please contact Colin Fox through:

> The Department of Extended Education
> (Extramural Studies Section)
> The University, London Road, READING RG1 5AQ
> from whom further copies of this booklet may be obtained.

Contents

Foreword   *iii*

Acknowledgements   *vi*

Preface   *vii*

Chapter 1   The road to the Somme   11

Chapter 2   The Battle of the Somme   13

Chapter 3   The 6th Battalion   17
Montauban 1 July   17
Delville Wood 19 July   26
Thiepval 26 September   31
Schwaben Redoubt 28 September   33

Chapter 4   The 5th Battalion   35
Ovillers 3 July   35
German counter-attack 8 August   42

Chapter 5   The 8th Battalion   45
Arrival on the Somme   45
Preparations for the attack on 14 July   46
Pearl Alley 14 July   47
Intermediate Line 18 August   49
High Wood 3 September   51

Chapter 6   After the battle: the old German line   55

Chapter 7   The cost of 1916   57

Chapter 8   The Somme: a postscript   59

Sources   60

Appendix I   Thirty men: brief biographies of some
of those who served with the battalions in 1916   62

Appendix II   The Somme battlefield today   76

Appendix III   Casualties and commemorations   81

Appendix IV   Honours and awards   92

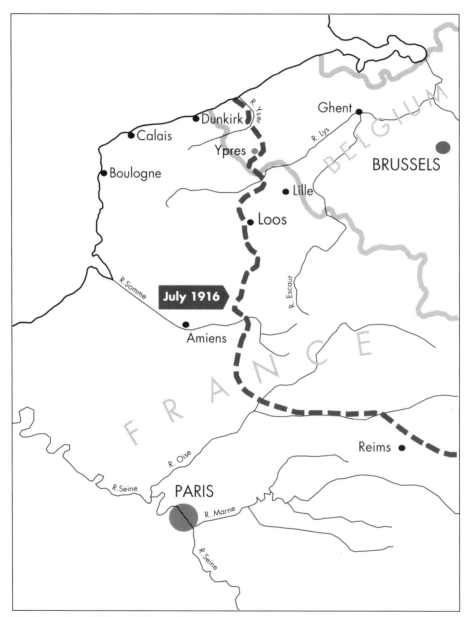

The Western Front: Belgium and Northern France

1   The road to the Somme

In response to the recruiting campaign launched on the outbreak of war by Lord Kitchener, the Royal Berkshire Regiment
had by early 1915 formed four 'Service' or 'Kitchener' battalions
which were intended for active service overseas. All the men
were volunteers: not only from Reading and Berkshire but drafts
brought in from London, South Wales and Birmingham. Of the
four battalions, one, the 7th, was to have only a short spell on
the Western Front before going on to spend most of the war in
Salonika. The other three, the 5th, 6th and 8th, were to see all
their service in France or Belgium – but with quite different
experiences of action, depending on the role played by the
infantry division of which they formed a part.

The 5th Battalion, after training at Shorncliffe, St Martin's
Plain and Folkestone, crossed to France with the 12th (Eastern)
Division on 30 May 1915. They then spent four months at
Ploegsteert in Belgium, ('Plug Street', as it was known to the
troops) where they were able to accustom themselves to the
rigours of trench warfare for some three months before going
into battle at Loos in October 1915.

The 6th Battalion trained at Colchester and Codford St Mary
with the 18th (Eastern) Division, like the 12th a Kitchener division, before embarking for France on 24 July 1915. They soon
found themselves in what was then the relatively quiet sector
of the Somme for their first experience of life in the trenches
which turned into an extended period of preparation for the
major offensive of 1916.

The 8th Battalion trained at Reading and then at Sutton Veney
near Warminster. What made their early experience so different
from that of the other two battalions was their subsequent allo-
cation to a Regular Army division, 1st Division, and their post-
ing to France on 7 August for an early encounter with the German army at the Battle of Loos on 25 September. A period of ini-
tiation was thus denied them and their first – and very heavy –
casualties came in a major action.

Hon. Lt & Quartermaster James Barrow, 8th Battalion Royal Berkshire Regiment, killed at the age of 47 near Loos on 1 June 1916 when a shell fell on the ration party he was leading to the trenches. Six of his party were also killed. They are buried in Noeux-les-Mines Communal Cemetery.

The first shared experience for the three battalions was the Battle of the Somme. In the months before the opening of the offensive on 1 July 1916, only the 6th Battalion had an extended period of familiarisation with the ground and with the opposing trench systems. After their arrival on the Somme in early August 1915 they were in and out of the line, suffering casualties from shell-fire and snipers, taking part in patrols and providing manual labour for mining parties. From March 1916 they trained and prepared for the coming attack.

In contrast, the 5th Battalion were well north of the Somme for the first half of 1916 in the Béthune-Loos-La-Bassée sector which had seen most of the fighting in the previous year. Here they rotated through from billets to front line relief and back again, not taking part in any major action but suffering casualties nevertheless. Their move with 12th Division to the Somme came on 16 June 1916 when they started a 10-day period of training for the offensive, going into trenches near Albert.

The 8th Battalion were the last to arrive on the Somme, moving into billets in Albert a week after the offensive opened. Like the 5th Battalion they had remained in the Loos sector for the early months of 1916, seeing action mainly in the form of trench raids. Their first experience of the Somme fighting was to come in mid-July.

These different roads to the Somme were to lead, as the following chapters show, to different kinds of participation in the offensive itself. The 6th Battalion were to be present virtually throughout the campaign, from the opening day to mid-November. The 5th Battalion, having attacked on 3 July, were not thereafter engaged in a major action on the Somme and they spent some five weeks out of the area, mainly at Arras, before returning to the Somme in early October. The 8th Battalion were involved in support actions during the period from mid-July to late September.

Before tracing the fortunes of the three battalions during the Battle of the Somme an introduction to the campaign itself is given.

2   The Battle of the Somme

The origins of the Battle of the Somme can be found in the proposal made on 29 December 1915 by General Joffre, Commander-in-Chief of the French Armies, to General Sir Douglas Haig, newly appointed Commander-in-Chief of the British Expeditionary Force, that a combined Franco-British offensive should take place on a 60-mile front astride the River Somme in the following year. Agreement to this proposal was confirmed on 14 February 1916 with 1 July as possible starting date. Haig's earlier preference for a campaign in Flanders was thus subordinated to the needs of the alliance, an echo of the decision which in September 1915 had resulted in the offensive at Loos.

The need for a major British involvement in 1916 became imperative when on 21 February the Germans attacked the French fortress town of Verdun. Relieving the pressure on the French army thus became one of the strategic aims of an offensive which lacked obvious territorial objectives.

The ground chosen for the joint offensive had seen no significant actions since 1914 and was relatively unspoilt. The countryside was open and undulating, dotted with woods and small villages. It was good campaigning country but with decided advantages for the defenders: high ground on the ridges gave excellent observation over attacking troops and chalky soil made possible deep dug-outs for protection against shell-fire. The Germans had had two years in which to make the most of these advantages. A forward defensive system had been constructed incorporating fortified villages whose names would become part of British history: Beaumont Hamel, Thiepval, Ovillers, La Boisselle, Fricourt, Mametz. A second system lay on the reverse slopes of high ground some 2,000 to 5,000 yards to the rear and a third was under construction. Both the first and the second systems were strongly wired.

To attack these positions a new British Army, the Fourth Army under Sir Henry Rawlinson, was created in February 1916 and detailed planning started in the following month. Eleven divisions of this army – some 120,000 men – were to be deployed on the first day, by now designated for 29 June. Of these, seven were New Army (Kitchener) divisions and four were drawn from the old Regular Army. To the north of them were three Territorial divisions, two of which from Third Army were to make a diversionary attack on the village of Gommecourt whilst the third held the line in between. The total attack frontage extended over 25,000 yards from Gommecourt down to Maricourt in the south. 18th Division and its right hand neighbour 30th Division were at this southern end of the front, adjoining the French Sixth Army.

Exactly what Fourth Army's objectives were to be in terms of ground to be taken had been a matter of some dispute between Haig and his Army Commander. Rawlinson favoured taking the German defensive systems one by one, on the so-called 'bite and hold' approach, whereas Haig saw a need to achieve an early breakthrough which could result in cavalry exploitation of a breach, with the German lines being 'rolled up' northwards. The objectives set for the opening day of the offensive seem to represent a compromise: in the north the German first and second positions were to be taken, in the south the first position and territory beyond up to a depth of two miles. Given the formidable German defences, the outcome would depend primarily on the effectiveness of the British (and French) preliminary artillery bombardment, timed to begin on 24 June, which to be successful had to destroy the barbed wire protecting the German trenches, had to kill or incapacitate the defenders and had to suppress the German artillery.

Compared with the weapons available to the British at the Battle of Loos progress had been made both in diversity and quantity. Trench mortars were now more reliable and available in greater numbers – as were hand grenades. Lewis light machine guns had been in regular service since late 1915. Although nearly three times as many artillery pieces – some 1,500 – were now available, a relatively small proportion were heavy guns, some of these of ancient vintage. Shells were still in limited supply and of the one and a half million fired in the 7-day preliminary bombardment (the attack date had to be postponed to 1 July because of unfavourable weather) one million were shrapnel shells – much less effective against deep defences than high explosive. The quality of the ammunition was also suspect; it has been estimated that between a quarter and a third of the shells fired failed to explode.

It was to a large extent due to this weakness in the destructive capacity of the artillery, combined with an over-optimistic esti-

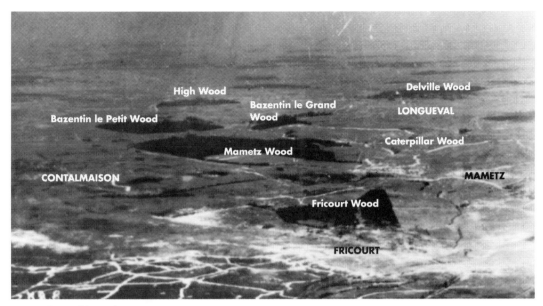

High Wood
Bazentin le Grand Wood
Delville Wood
LONGUEVAL
Bazentin le Petit Wood
Caterpillar Wood
Mametz Wood
CONTALMAISON
MAMETZ
Fricourt Wood
FRICOURT

An aerial view of the southern sector of the Somme battlefield on 1 July 1916 (PRO)

mation of its likely effectiveness, that the opening day of the offensive was an almost unmitigated disaster. Almost, because in the southern sector on the 18th and 30th Division front, where creeping barrages were used more effectively than elsewhere and where the German artillery was weaker, all objectives were taken. On most of the front no ground was gained, many of the attacks foundering before the German wire. The casualties sustained – 19,240 killed, 35,493 wounded and 2,152 missing, according to the Official Historian, – remain the worst suffered by the British Army in any single day of battle.

That a different approach could be successful was demonstrated some two weeks later when on 14 July, after a short intensive bombardment, some 6,000 yards of the German second position in the south was captured by troops who had been assembled in the darkness, some to within 200 yards or less of the German lines.

Through the remainder of July and August attempts were made to exploit this success, most of them foundering with heavy casualties on both sides against strongly held German positions in villages and woods. The third German position was attacked on 15 September, using tanks for the first time in warfare, and gains in ground were made, without a breakthrough being achieved. Thereafter, with notable exceptions such as the capture of Thiepval on 27 September and of Beaumont Hamel on 13 November, the campaign as a whole stagnated and finally succumbed to the deteriorating weather.

15

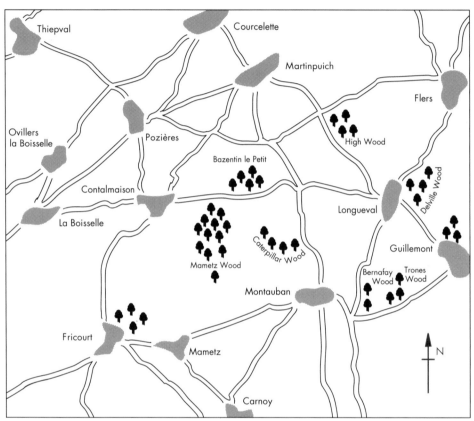

Thiepval

Courcelette

Martinpuich

Flers

Ovillers
la Boisselle

Pozières

High Wood

Bazentin le Petit

Contalmaison

Longueval

Delville Wood

La Boisselle

Caterpillar Wood

Guillemont

Mametz Wood

Bernafay
Wood

Trones
Wood

Montauban

N

Fricourt

Mametz

Carnoy

The sector of the Somme battlefield in
which the actions of the Royal Berkshire
battalions took place

Scale: 1:80,000

3 The 6th Battalion

**Montauban
1 July**

The 6th Battalion had been in the Somme area since August 1915 and it began training in March 1916 for the July offensive. On 21 May Lieutenant-Colonel BG Clay took over command. The battalion was part of 53rd Brigade in 18th Division, a New Army division which in this, its first battle, was to gain a high reputation for performance based on thorough preparation and training. The Divisional Commander was Major-General Ivor Maxse, who in 1917 would be promoted to the command of an Army Corps and who would end the war as Inspector-General of Training.

General Maxse's 'doctrine' as it applied to 18th Division's preparation for the Somme battles is summarised in a report he wrote in December 1916 which contains the following exhortation:

> 'Teach, drill and practise a definite form of attack so that every man shall know it thoroughly. On the basis of theory and knowledge common to all, any brigade, battalion or company commander varies his attack formation to suit any condition which may be peculiar to his front and to his objective. The reason for this system is that all ranks know at least one attack formation thoroughly. It can be varied according to circumstance and at short notice.'

In their preparations for the attack on 1 July 1916 XIII Corps, to which 18th Division belonged, had arranged that all their troops would train over ground where a complete set of model trenches had been dug, reproduced from aerial photographs and representing in exact detail the German trenches to be attacked. References in the 6th Battalion's War Diary confirm the Royal Berkshires' participation in this training:

> '9 May 1916: Battalion went to Poulainville to dig new model trenches.
> 12 May 1916: To Poulainville to practise attack. Haig inspected training.'

A private in the battalion who later deposited his reminiscences with the Imperial War Museum was Fred Henwood. He was a Reading man, a painter by trade, who enlisted in November

17

1915 and served with the 6th Battalion until 1917 when he was severely wounded and discharged from the army. He wrote about the period of training:

> 'The battalion had been holding the line at Carnoy for a few months before the attack came off. They had come out of the line for three months training for the attack.... One nice summer's day had a sham attack with aeroplanes, with a little signalling light fixed to the aeroplane and dropping messages. The aeroplanes also had a mock battle above our heads.'

For the opening of the offensive 18th Division were located on the right or southern end of the British line, close to the boundary with the French army. Ahead and just to the right of the 6th Battalion's line of attack was the village of Montauban on the crest of a ridge. Beyond and directly ahead lay Caterpillar Wood and Caterpillar Valley which marked the limits of the planned advance on the first day of the battle. The ground in front of the Berkshires was, in the words of the British Official History, 'a long gentle slope, on the right almost flat.'

The site of Montauban village
July 1916 (IWM Q4003)

Maxse was disposing his division in a novel way by having all three of his brigades, rather than two, attack in line. Each brigade would be spearheaded by two battalions and so six assault battalions would be launched to gain and hold the furthest objectives. The 6th Royal Berkshires were to be one of these.

On this sector of the front the preparatory bombardment which had started on 24 June was successful in that the German wire had largely been destroyed and considerable damage had been caused to trench defences. This was unfortunately not true for much of the line to the north.

German guns were also firing before the offensive started and the 6th Battalion lost 6 men killed and 72 wounded between 27 June and 1 July. These losses were attributed at least partly to the inadequacy of the dug-outs in which the men were waiting. As Private Henwood remembered:

> 'During the 6-day bombardment we were on carrying parties, carrying 60-pound trench mortars up to the front line. At night we were carrying up rations and also unloading ammunition and aerial torpedoes, which were the size of an orange box. One or two of our dug-outs had been smashed in and the men were buried and had to be dug out, some dead.'

Captain RA Rochfort, Adjutant to the battalion, wrote in a memoir contributed to the regimental history about his impressions of the days immediately before the attack:

> 'This period of holding the line was the most extraordinary one imaginable. Throughout the day it was quite safe to walk about the front line, sit up on the trenches, look over the German line and watch the shelling without any fear of being sniped at. The country in front of our barbed wire appeared absolutely devoid of German life; the German guns only replied at night and then replied to very good effect. Rifle-shot in the daytime was an unheard-of thing.'

At 3.00 am on 1 July the battalion moved into its assembly trenches. It had been arranged that each man would be given hot tea or soup and a bully beef sandwich up to an hour before the attack. Instructions had also been given, perhaps unnecessarily, that there would be no cheering when the men left their lines so as not to let the Germans know they were coming.

Each man was to carry his rifle and equipment without his

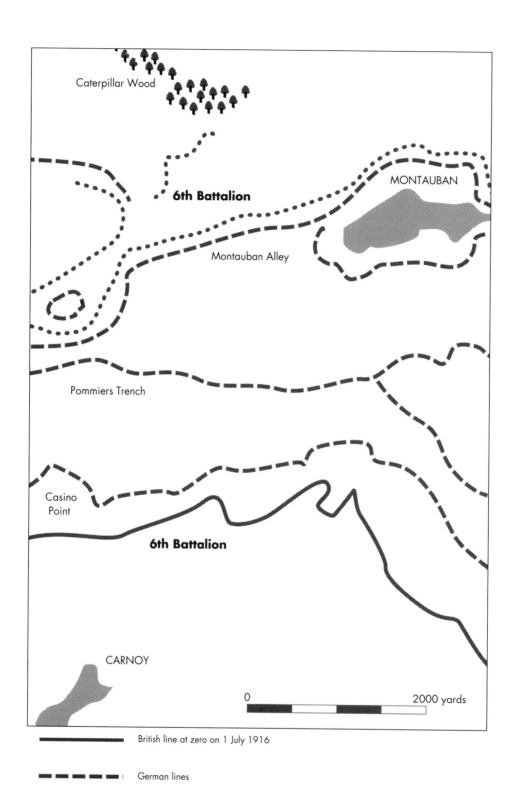

Caterpillar Wood

6th Battalion

MONTAUBAN

Montauban Alley

Pommiers Trench

Casino
Point

6th Battalion

CARNOY

0   2000 yards

——————— British line at zero on 1 July 1916

▬ ▬ ▬ ▬ ▬ German lines

• • • • • • • • • British line gained and held at night

pack but with 170 rounds of ammunition, a haversack containing two tins of meat, eight hard biscuits and a grocery ration, a waterproof sheet, a jersey, two Mills bombs, two sandbags (empty) and two smoke helmets. As far as possible, officers were to change into other ranks' uniform to make them less of a target for German snipers.

The total attacking strength of the battalion was 20 officers (the maximum permitted) and 656 other ranks. In comparison, their brigade neighbours who were going into action on their right, the 8th Norfolks, likewise had 20 officers but were over 200 men stronger with 896 other ranks.

The 6th Battalion's objectives for the day were firstly a German reserve trench known as Pommiers Trench lying some 1,000 yards from the British line and secondly a German communication trench, Montauban Alley, a further 1,000 yards away. Thereafter a shorter distance would need to be covered to establish an advanced line overlooking Caterpillar Wood and giving observation over the German positions in Caterpillar Valley.

At 7.27 am the first two waves of the leading companies under Captain S Fenner and Captain R Litten went over the parapet and formed up in front of the trenches. At 7.28 am a British mine which had been laid under a German machine gun nest, Casino Point, exploded, its falling debris causing some casualties in the first attacking waves. Captain Rochfort witnessed the explosion:

> 'The machine guns at Casino Point were doing quite a bit of damage when suddenly there was a blinding flash; the whole of the earth seemed to shake and the mine went up. The air was filled with large lumps of earth, Germans, machine-guns, baulks of wood, concrete emplacements and all the debris of the strong point itself. The crater was forty feet deep and quite thirty yards across.'

Another witness was Private Fred Henwood who testified to the demoralisation of the German defenders when relating how 'six big Germans', including an officer, surrendered without a fight to him and three of his pals.

The battalion's first objective, Pommiers Trench, was reached by 7.50 am. It was here that the the first serious German resistance was encountered, principally from machine gunners, and the battalion's heaviest losses of the day were suffered whilst the position was being consolidated. Captain Litten was killed, as were Lieutenant Traill and Second Lieutenant Collot. Captain McArthur was wounded and Second Lieutenant Courage was ordered to move up and take over command of 'B' Company which now had no officers left. The 8th Norfolks on the right had been held up and Captain Fenner organised three bombing squads to protect the exposed flank, attaching a Lewis Gun to each. With the flank secured, the advance on the second objective, Montauban Alley, could begin and by 12.50 pm about half the length of this trench was in British hands.

Fighting now became very disconnected, consisting of bombing attacks supported by mortars rather than of successive waves of riflemen. Progress was slow, a particular source of difficulty being a German sniper using an automatic rifle. Attempts were made to bomb him but without success. Lieutenant Rushton of the Brigade Mortar Battery tried to shoot him with his revolver but was himself killed. Thereupon Second Lieutenant Saye of the 6th Royal Berkshires went out with a rifle but he too was fatally wounded. Finally, Company Sergeant-Major Sayer jumped on to the parapet and fired at the sniper at the same time as the latter fired at him. Company Sergeant-Major Sayer killed the sniper but was severely wounded himself. For this action he was awarded the Distinguished Conduct Medal. It was not until 4.45 pm, when mortars had been brought up into Montauban Alley, that the Germans finally retired and the position could be consolidated.

The battalion's final objective overlooking Caterpillar Wood was taken and partially consolidated by 6.30 pm, marking an advance for the day of some 2,500 yards. This was an exceptional achievement matched only by units of the 30th Division on the right – and by the French Sixth Army to their right. At 4.00 pm on the following day the battalion was relieved by the 8th Suffolks and went into rest until 7 July.

Reflecting on the first day's attack General Maxse wrote in a report dated 18 August:

> 'It is of interest to note that the left battalion of the centre brigade (i.e. the 6th Royal Berkshires) reached Pommiers Trench in less than 20 minutes, whereas the right battalion (i.e. the 8th Norfolks) reached the same line several hours later. Both battalions encountered stout opposition and both fought hard and suffered heavy casualties, but of the two I should say that the one on the left which went quicker had the severer task. The quick moving battalion followed its

barrage close up; the slower battalion lost touch with its barrage in 10 minutes. This was owing to the different German
dispositions in the two localities.'

The reference to different German dispositions is explained by
the fact that the German regimental commander opposite the
8th Norfolks kept his strength forward whereas his colleague
opposite the 6th Royal Berkshires put his strength in the rear
trenches.

In addition to Private Henwood another private in the 6th
Battalion who left an account of his service was AJ Gosling. He
enlisted at Abingdon in December 1914 and served throughout
the war. His view of the attack on 1 July and its aftermath is
that of a member of a carrying party:

'On 1 July at 7.00 am the guns were very busy. It was an ideal
day for the attack, a light fog mingling with the smoke screen.
At 7.30 am we had the order to advance. At the front line I
had the sad experience of seeing two mates in front of me
fall but I still carried on, passing a good many wounded men
on the way. After dodging the shells I reached the German
front line safely. Here we were able to get a little lower,
although the trenches had been terribly knocked about and
a good many German dead were lying there.

After we had been called together we started for our objective where we were to leave our bombs and ammunition, but
on arriving volunteers were called for to take ammunition
and bombs to the boys in the front trench.

We were then ordered to hang on till the next night, so we
all took our place to ward off any counter-attack. By this time
the Germans had got the range of our position and were
shelling it rather heavily, but we got out the next day, having
carried food and water to the front area quite safely, and
returned to Carnoy. The next day we were formed into burial
parties. I was in charge of our party and it fell to my lot to
bury my own section, men that I had served with since joining the battalion.'

The 35th Brigade Commander, Brigadier-General HW Higginson, also had a story to tell about the day after the battle. On 2
July he was returning to Montauban when he saw a group of
men collected around a dug-out from which smoke was issuing.
They were trying to bomb out a German who had been sniping
from there for 24 hours and had wounded three men in the legs
as they passed. There was only one entrance to the dug-out but

smoke bombs and grenades thrown in had no effect. On the following day the entrance was blown in and the German was left to die of starvation or thirst. It was assumed that he had constructed a barricade across the dug-out behind which he could take refuge when bombs were thrown. General Maxse who included this incident in his report of 18 August saw it as evidence that the Germans were not showing signs of demoralisation after the British advance.

Some of the reasons for the success of the attack on 1 July were identified by Captain Fenner writing as Commanding Officer in the battalion War Diary on 30 July 1916:

'The success of this operation was due to the thorough grounding everyone had in his work. The whole scheme had been explained to the men and even when the majority of the officers had been knocked out, the NCOs and men carried on according to programme. Every man knew the ground from the excellent maps that were received and this assisted in the successful attainment of the objective.'

Brigadier-General Higginson subsequently set out in the brigade War Diary his reasons which included:

- careful preparation of the ground from which the attack was launched
- previous training over trenches which were an exact facsimile of the German trenches
- effective artillery preparation and wire cutting
- co-operation of artillery during the attack.

Amplification of this praise of the artillery can be found in a letter received at Fourth Army Headquarters from the General Officer Commanding XIII Corps drawing attention to the excellent services rendered by French artillery both in the preliminary bombardments and in counter battery work. XIII Corps' two divisions, the 18th and the 30th, were the beneficiaries of the French XX Corps artillery on their right.

When the volume of the Official British History covering the opening of the Somme offensive was being compiled after the war, its author Brigadier-General Sir James Edmonds sent drafts for comment to officers who had taken part in the operations. One of his correspondents, MF Grove-White, wrote on 10 January 1931 that in his opinion – formed at the time:

'Extreme care was taken to foresee and provide for every

possible eventuality and not to rely solely on a set piece attack worked out according to a programme.... In training for the attack great attention was paid in 18th Division to training in open warfare methods i.e. troops working forward by fire and manoeuvre without artillery support.'

This view was supported by another correspondent, EG Miles of 54th Brigade writing on 30 April 1930, who regarded the intensive training and the effect of the preliminary bombardment as being the two main factors.

Despite all the thorough preparation and the subsequent success of the operations on 1 July, casualties in the 6th Royal Berkshires were high. They were reported at the time as:
Officers killed
    Capt R Litten, Lt KR Traill, 2nd Lt E Bayly, 2nd Lt TA Collot,
    2nd Lt GM Courage, 2nd Lt CK Howe, 2nd Lt NB Souper.
Officers wounded
    Capt HGF Longhurst, Capt VG McArthur,
    2nd Lt JV McLean, 2nd Lt GWH Nicholson, 2nd Lt LH Saye.
Other ranks casualties
    71 killed, 254 wounded, 11 missing.

In concluding this account of the 6th Battalion's performance on 1 July it is worth recalling both Haig's cautious words spoken at a conference held at Fourth Army Headquarters on 22 June 1916:
    'We must remember however that we are working with New
    Army troops and that unfortunately we have not got those
    fine fellows we had at the beginning of the war, imbued
    with the discipline of the army and its great traditions.'
and Rawlinson's message to Maxse of 2 July:
    'Please convey to 18th Division best congratulations and
    thank them for their dashing attack yesterday. They have
    done excellent work and I desire to thank them most
    heartily.'

Delville Wood
19 July

After what was on most of the front a disastrously unsuccessful start to the Somme offensive, an imaginatively-planned and well-executed attack on 14 July against part of the German second-line positions enabled British forces to secure the Longueval-Bazentin ridge north of Montauban.

At 7.00 pm on 18 July the 6th Battalion, now with a fighting strength of 19 officers and 401 other ranks, received orders to move from their position south of Carnoy to take part in an action the following day at Longueval and Delville Wood. For this operation they and their colleagues in 53rd Brigade came under the command of the 9th (Scottish) Division whose South African Brigade had just been forced out of the northern part of the village and most of Delville Wood in a series of German counter-attacks.

The 53rd Brigade attack was to be led by the 8th Norfolks who were to clear the southern part of Delville Wood from its western edge. This having been done, the 6th Royal Berkshires and the 10th Essex would clear the northern part of the wood whilst the 8th Suffolks took back the northern part of Longueval.

The plans for this operation were not given to the 53rd Brigade Commander until 12.30 am on 19 July. The Royal Berkshires

Delville Wood, September 1916
(IWM Q1211)

were alerted at 3.30 am by their Commanding Officer and were ready to move off half an hour later. However, a proposed start for the 8th Norfolks at 6.15 am had to be delayed by an hour because of the difficulties experienced in assembling their troops. Their attack then had to be launched without artillery support.

The Royal Berkshires finally began to move up to the line at 7.05 am. It was now light and the Germans started to shell the area, one shell falling on a battalion carrying-party and killing five men. According to Captain Fenner's after-action report, 34 men were killed getting up to the village, although this figure does not tally with the day's registered casualties. Progress was further hindered by troops coming back from Longueval on relief and partially blocking the road.

Captain Rochfort described this move up to Longueval in his memoir:

'The four battalions were sent up through a defile (the sunken road into Longueval) in broad daylight, with German balloons up, and most of the battalion had to halt for quite a considerable period in the sunken road, where they were exposed to shelling from three sides. Every gun that the Germans could get turned on to the road opened fire, and I have never seen a short stretch of road with so many casualties on it as the piece leading into Longueval village.'

The 6th Battalion reached the outskirts of the village at 9.00 am and here they waited for a signal from the Norfolks that the southern portion of Delville Wood had been cleared. This came at 11.40 am and the battalion, now further weakened by the effects of enemy artillery and machine gun fire, moved through the southern part of the village into the wood. However, because of continued German resistance, their move northwards through the wood could not start until 1.30 pm.

Their attack was preceded by a half hour bombardment, some of it falling short, but the Royal Berkshires and the 10th Essex still met with very stiff resistance. Little progress was made beyond 'Princes Street', a ride running west–east through the wood and dividing it approximately at the half way point. At 2.15 pm they were ordered to consolidate and by 3.30 pm a line running some 120 yards south of Princes Street had been established. This line was held in the face of numerous counterattacks until the two battalions were relieved at 2.00 am on 21 July. According to the historian of the 18th Division, the Royal

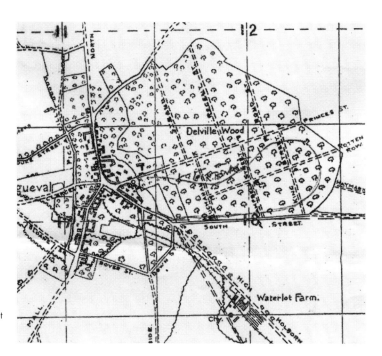

This 1916 map of Longueval and Delville Wood shows the section of the wood south of Princes Street occupied by the 6th Battalion on 19 July

Berkshires received no food supplies the whole of the time they were in the wood.

This same historian gives a glimpse of one of the most celebrated members of the 6th Battalion, namely Captain Harold Ackroyd of the Royal Army Medical Corps who was attached to the battalion as medical officer and who was later awarded the Military Cross for his conduct on 1 July:

'Captain Ackroyd was a heroic figure during those two days. The fighting was so confused and the wood so hard to search that the difficulties of evacuating the wounded seemed unconquerable. But Captain Ackroyd, bespectacled and stooping, a Cambridge don before he joined the forces, was so cool, purposeful and methodical, that he cleared the whole wood of wounded, British and Boche as well.'

In the following year, during the opening days of the Third Battle of Ypres, Captain Ackroyd was to sacrifice his life for those in his care and be awarded a posthumous Victoria Cross.

An infantryman's view of the confusion of this action was given by Private TA Jennings, a Lewis Gunner in the 6th Battalion, in a memoir written in 1966 and deposited with the Imperial War Museum:

'We reached a communication trench running alongside the

28

road with a wood the other side. As Captain Hudson was talking to the regimental sergeant-major a German sniper saw them, killed the regimental sergeant-major and put a bullet through the captain's tin hat.

At last we came to the end of the trench. Our captain was there to give us the signal when to go (across to the road). "Follow your sergeant – go!" The sergeant shot across the road as if from a gun; each man ran singly under withering machine-gun fire and shelling. I did not see a single man falter.

Captain Hudson followed suit but lost the sergeant and myself in the wood. I wandered around for a moment or so and then dived into a shell hole. A couple of our lads appeared and asked me what I was doing. I got out of the hole and we set off in the direction we thought we should go. With a bit of luck we ran into a platoon of soldiers who turned out to be South Africans. They indicated to us where they thought our company was. We eventually found them at the edge of the wood.

The wood was littered with hundreds of wounded and dying men. We received no food supplies the whole time we were in there. The air was thick with the horrible stench from the dead bodies and the pungent odour of gas. The "Devil's Wood" was truly a terrible place...'

The verdict of a member of the 10th Essex, RA Chell, was conveyed to Sir James Edmonds in 1933 in response to his request for comments on the preliminary draft of the Official History:

'The 53rd Brigade was lent to another division in a foolishly precipitate manner. No thought was given to the question of breakfasts on the 19th. The infantry plan of attack was poor and its execution, as conceived, impossible. Forward movement and deployment of a whole brigade was carried out in daylight and under direct and close terrestrial observation, machine-gun and rifle fire and enfilade artillery fire.'

Royal Berkshire casualties during the operation, mainly from artillery and machine-gun fire, were heavy, approximately forty percent of the battalion, according to its diarist, being killed or wounded in the opening six hours. For 19/20 July the casualties were reported as:
Officers killed
2nd Lt WV Burgess, 2nd Lt CJ Fuller, 2nd Lt HP Sadler.

Officers wounded

    Capt AH Hudson, 2nd Lt AJ Fox, 2nd Lt CH Hunt,
    2nd Lt JN Richardson.
    In addition 2nd Lt SR Collier was missing.

Other ranks casualties

    27 killed, 127 wounded, 30 missing.

In a report written after the operation the Brigade Commander enumerated the reasons as he saw them for the failure of the brigade to take its objectives. Among them were:

- insufficient time for preparation and reconnaissance
- troops having to move up in daylight and being exposed to enemy fire
- congestion caused by reliefs going on when attacking battalions were moving up
- the delay in the start of the attack
- commanders and troops not being trained to carry out difficult tasks at short notice
- difficulties of communication between brigade and battalions.

These perceived weaknesses contrast sharply with the acknowledged strengths of 18th Division's 'set-piece' operation on 1 July. On 19 July a quickly improvised small-scale attack failed in conditions which perhaps demanded too much of command as well as of the men. A remarkably frank telephone message was received at Haig's headquarters at 7.50 am on 19 July stating that Fourth Army did not know who was in command either at Longueval or at Montauban and neither did XIII Corps. All wires appeared to be cut and the only communication possible was by runner. Haig's somewhat starchy response was: 'I do not think this indicates sufficient method. In order to win, the first essential is to organise a sound system of command.'

For the 6th Royal Berkshires the two July operations meant virtually the end of the battalion as it was originally recruited. Because of the need to reconstitute the battalion almost from scratch, it could not be used again during the Somme offensive in other than a supporting role.

**Thiepval
26 September**

Thiepval village, and the ridge on which it lies, had been a first day objective of the Somme offensive. In common with most of the German defensive positions in the central and the northern sectors of the front, it had resisted capture on 1 July and it remained for almost three months an important point of observation across the British lines.

The 18th Division was given the task of taking both Thiepval and the German strong-point known as the Schwaben Redoubt which lay to the north. For three weeks before the attack, which was scheduled for 26 September, the division engaged in a daily routine of practice and gained a thorough familiarity with the ground to be taken. This time the attack on the village, by now in ruins, would come from the south with supporting enfilade artillery fire from the west. Testimony to the thoroughness of the preparations is contained in the report compiled by Major-General Maxse in December 1916 to which reference was made earlier. The Official Historian describes the men as being 'in fine fettle' after their three weeks' battle training.

The 8th Suffolks were to lead the attack together with the 10th Essex. The 8th Norfolks were in support whilst the 6th Royal Berkshires remained behind in brigade reserve. After three days of preliminary bombardment zero hour came at 12.35 pm on 26 September, a time chosen by Maxse to allow some, but not too many, daylight hours for consolidation which would then continue under the cover of darkness. No Man's Land was some 250 yards wide on this part of the front and the first objective, Thiepval village, lay 1,000 yards ahead. The German front line was crossed without difficulty, enemy troops appearing, according to the Official History, eager to surrender without fighting. The remains of Thiepval village, with the exception of its north-west corner, were taken and after an hour's halt the advance was resumed towards the Schwaben Redoubt a further 1,000 yards away. Now progress was much more difficult, the 10th Essex in particular encountering stiff resistance from the German-held position in Thiepval village not cleared by the neighbouring brigade. The advance finally came to a standstill and at 6.20 pm further operations were postponed until the next day.

The 6th Battalion now had the task of providing carrying parties which struggled through the night to bring fresh water, food and ammunition to the exhausted troops at the front. Private Jennings gives an account of what this entailed:
'We were in reserve dug-outs at Crucifix Corner. Then it was

our turn and we made our way forward in small columns to Thiepval, unmolested, in broad daylight. Dusk was creeping up fast and then came the biggest barrage Jerry ever sent over; this went on throughout the hours of darkness till dawn.

The trench we were in must have been a terrible hot spot during the past few weeks, for buried in its walls were dozens of bodies, both British and German, rotting in the earth. That evening and throughout the night the 6th Berkshires worked in parties carrying food, water, ammunition and stores to the forward line where the troops awaited their arrival with eagerness.

Daylight gave us the opportunity of looking further afield. A huge crater came into our view about 50 yards away. The occupants were the dead of the soldiers who made the advance on 1 July, nearly three months before. We were about to retreat to the trench when our captain came across to reprimand us for being away from our position. Then he ordered us to search the bodies for their personal belongings, paybooks etc. This helped to clear up the "Missing believed killed" problem. We found that they were Dorsets. It wasn't a pleasant task.'

Captain Rochfort also had memories of going up to the front line in this sector:

'The general line here faced north and the communication trenches were really two old German communication trenches between Thiepval and Schwaben. There were no traverses in either of these trenches and both were in view from the Schwaben Redoubt. As a consequence, a visit to the front line was a most unpleasant affair. Add to this the fact that the Germans attempted to bomb down these trenches three or four times a day and that they were well supplied with egg bombs, while our supply of Mills bombs, which were the only reply to an egg bomb, was very limited and it will be realised that the days we spent holding Thiepval were somewhat exciting.'

6th Battalion casualties for 26/27 September were reported as: 1 other rank killed and 11 wounded.

Schwaben Redoubt 28 September

The renewed attack on the Schwaben Redoubt was timed for 1.00 pm on 28 September. The 6th Royal Berkshires were again in brigade reserve and were located in Authuille Wood. The assault battalions gained a footing in the Redoubt by 2.30 pm, after suffering heavy casualties, and by 5.00 pm the 8th Suffolks had reached the final objective.

Early German counter-attacks on the following morning led to ground being lost and the 6th Battalion were sent up at dawn to relieve the Suffolks. They were heavily shelled all day, many of the men suffering, according to the battalion diarist, from want of sleep. Over the next few days spasmodic bombing attacks were carried out by both sides in deteriorating weather which, together with the heavy shelling, reduced the ground to a sea of mud. By the time that the 18th Division was relieved by the 39th on 5 October most of the Redoubt was back in British hands. On 6 October the Royal Berkshires were withdrawn from the line and moved into billets.

6th Battalion casualties for the period 28 September to October were reported as:
Officers killed
    2nd Lt AD Beebee (30-9-16), 2nd Lt GC Freeman (1-10-16),
    2nd Lt GP Ravenor (2-10-16).
Officers wounded
    Maj J Crookenden DSO (30-9-16),
    Lt GSC Welch (3-10-16), 2nd Lt WB Chapman (29-9-16).
Other ranks
    14 killed, 147 wounded, 15 missing.

Thereafter the battalion was engaged with 18th Division in successful actions north-west of Courcelette at Regina Trench on 21 October and at Desire Trench on 18 November.

Some impression of what the fighting during the Somme offensive meant, as far as the composition of the 6th Battalion is concerned, can perhaps be conveyed by the following statistics:
Battalion parapet strength on 24 June 1916
    officers: 18
    other ranks: 754.
Reinforcements received from 24 June to 27 November
    officers: 20
    other ranks: 924.
Parapet strength on 27 November 1916
    officers: 26
    other ranks: 607.

On 7 November 1916 Major-General Maxse presented gallantry
awards to the following members of the battalion:
Military Cross to
    2nd Lt AHT Lewis, (for work with the battalion bombers
    at Thiepval).
Distinguished Conduct Medal to
    CSM R Ruffell.
Military Medal to
    10 other ranks.

The battalion spent the last weeks of 1916 with 18th Division
in rest billets in the Abbeville area.

4 The 5th Battalion

Ovillers
3 July 1916

On 1 July the 5th Battalion moved to Albert where 12th Division were to relieve 8th Division in the front line trenches. On arriving there the trenches were found to be, according to the battalion diarist, 'in a filthy state with dead and wounded lying about.'

On the following evening orders were received for a divisional attack at dawn on 3 July to take the village of Ovillers. This had been a first day objective on the opening of the Somme offensive but had resisted capture. Zero hour was set for 3.15 am and it was to be preceded by a one hour's bombardment.

The leading waves of the two battalions in 35th Brigade making the attack (the 5th Royal Berkshires and the 7th Suffolks) in fact started to crawl forward at 3.03 am to reduce their assaulting dis-

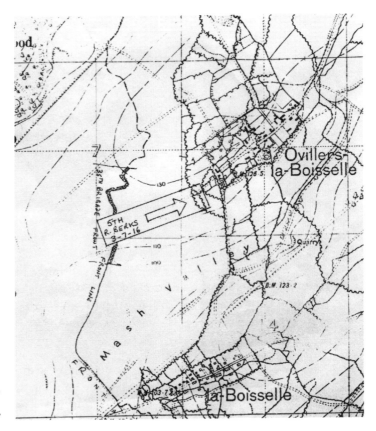

Section of a 1916 trench map showing the direction of the 5th Battalion's attack on 3 July

35

Extract from Lt-Col Willan's entry in the 5th Battalion War Diary

tance. Behind them there was some congestion in the assembly trenches and a German counter-bombardment caused casualties amongst the men waiting to move up. The initial advance went well and in darkness, dust and smoke the German front line trench was reached with few casualties. The main obstacles here were large shell holes; the German wire on the other hand had been almost completely destroyed.

The assault troops passed over the German front line trench, which appeared to be only lightly held, crossed the second trench and moved on to the third, 'Shrapnel Terrace', which ran near the village. This line contained a great many deep dug-outs from which the German defenders had to be forced out with grenades. Hand-to-hand fighting followed with bombing parties from each side confronting each other in the remains of the trench, the advantage resting with the Germans who had plentiful supplies of grenades. The Royal Berkshires' bombers soon found themselves isolated and running out of supplies. By 9.00 am, according to the British Official History, 12th Division was reporting total failure with the exception of a footing gained in the outskirts of Ovillers which in the end was lost. The 5th Battalion diarist stated that there was 'no doubt that some men penetrated as far as the village and were eventually killed or cut off.'

An eye-witness account of actions between the German lines was published in the *Reading Mercury* on 29 July 1916. Colour-Sergeant William Rixon of Wargrave told the press:

> 'When we got between the second and third German lines, the Germans opened a rapid fire, using in addition plenty of bombs. Lieutenant Brown was killed early on, receiving wounds in each leg, both arms and stomach, whilst Captain Stewart was killed by a shell in the first line. The enemy machine-guns were murderous and no one could have lived in it. Many of our poor fellows were being killed as they lay in the field, wounded and helpless, by the enemy's machine-guns which swept over them.... I myself was struck when I got to the wire in the second line, being hit with shrapnel, but was fortunate enough to get back.'

Lt Gold

Some of the survivors retired to the German front line, by then almost totally obliterated, where, as German machine-gun fire was still causing heavy casualties, they sought cover in shell holes. They were joined here by the Battalion Commander, Lieutenant-Colonel Willan, and the Adjutant, Lieutenant Cecil Gold, who had gone forward when the last waves left the start trenches. The only other officer present appeared to be Captain Wace who was trying to rally the men and get them to go forward. When German troops were seen to be advancing in strength and realising that he was exposed to attacks from the front and from both flanks, Lieutenant-Colonel Willan made the decision to withdraw to the shelter of a sunken road which led from Ovillers in the direction of Albert and here some 100 men entrenched themselves. It was on this sunken road that Lieutenant Gold was killed, as Lieutenant-Colonel Willan described in a letter he wrote to the family two days later:

'As soon as all the companies had gone, I went forward to the German trenches with Cecil and my orderly, who was, I believe, also killed. Cecil and I ran about trying to restore matters as there was some confusion in the darkness, and trying to get the men to dig themselves in along the sunken road. He was killed on the road and died instantaneously as he was shot by a rifle bullet through the brain.'

The troops could not be reinforced in this position because of heavy German artillery and machine-gun fire and under cover of darkness they were withdrawn. They were later joined in the defence lines near Albert by a party of about 50 men under Second Lieutenants Breach and May who had been dug in in No Man's Land.

An incident which occurred during the withdrawal was described by Lieutenant-Colonel Willan in his report made to 35th Brigade the following day. An order to retire was apparently given by an officer from another unit. One NCO thought that the order actually came from a German masquerading in British uniform. 'Whoever it was', wrote Lieutenant-Colonel Willan, 'was shot, it is believed, by Captain Wace with his revolver.'

Lieutenant Breach's account of his part in the action was published in the *Berkshire Chronicle* on 16 May 1919:
'I have had the most thrilling and certainly most terrible time I should imagine it is possible for anyone to go through and remain sane. We attacked the Huns at 3.00 am on the 3rd July. We managed to take the Hun lines, but after some heroic work on the part of our fellows, the battalion was driven off. We found it totally impossible to get back to our own lines, so we had to lie down in the open, exposed to the fire of both the Hun's artillery and our own, to say nothing of Fritz's rifle fire, machine-gun fire and bombs, for 20 hours. We crept back in after dark. Of our officers only the Battalion Commander and two second lieutenants, of whom I am one, got back. I was buried once by a "Jack Johnson" (German shell). Those 20 hours seemed quite a week to me.'

The failure of the attacking troops to hold the ground they had taken was attributed by Lieutenant-Colonel Willan to:
- the intense darkness, made worse by the dust and smoke which hung near the trenches
- the noise of the artillery and machine-gun bombardment which made it impossible to hear orders

- the depth of the German dug-outs (30 to 40 feet) which enabled the troops in them to survive the bombardment
- an inadequate supply of bombs
- the very heavy casualties amongst officers and senior NCOs which occurred early in the attack, some of them from land mines laid between the first and second German lines and detonated by trip wires.

The verdict of the British Official History amplifies this analysis of a costly and unsuccessful day's operation:

'The action, which cost nearly 2,400 officers and men (of 12th Division) was another reminder that an assault upon a narrow front, without adequate flank protection and lacking the element of surprise, was bound to result in a useless waste of lives. For the infantry to have reached the German trenches at all was an outstanding feat of arms.'

A survivor of the 5th Battalion's attack was Private H Harding and he expressed his views laconically in a post-war memoir:

'Our attack at Ovillers proved abortive, only killed and wounded to show for our efforts. Afterwards we were assembled in a field near Mametz Wood, where our Brigadier, Solly Flood, told us that war was a bloody rough game calling for bloody rough action. As if we didn't know!'

Bringing in wounded men on the Albert-Bapaume road near La Boisselle, 3 July 1916 (IWM Q770)

Another post-war account, *A Subaltern's War* by Charles Edmonds, contains a description of the Ovillers battlefield two weeks after the 5th Battalion's attack:

> 'The western and southern slopes of the village had been comparatively little shelled; that is, a little grass had still room to grow between the shell holes. The village was guarded by tangle after tangle of rusty barbed wire in irregular lines. Among the wire lay rows of khaki figures, as they had fallen to the machine-guns on the crest, thick as the sleepers in the Green Park on a summer Sunday evening. The simile leapt to my mind at once of flies on a fly paper. I did not know then that twice in the fortnight before our flank attack, had a division been hurled at that wire-encircled hill, and twice had it withered away before hidden machine-guns.'

5th Battalion casualties in the attack on 3 July were initially reported as:
Officers killed or died of wounds
Capt H Stewart, Capt PB Wace,
Lt CA Gold, 2nd Lt AEW Butler.
In addition 3 officers were wounded and 7 reported missing.
Other ranks casualties
2 killed, 212 wounded, 104 missing.

The final total of those killed was in fact 89.

On 6 July the battalion strength was reported as 340 all ranks and on this day Cecil Gold was buried in Aveluy Cemetery. His brother Pat later wrote about the moment when the family received the news of Cecil's death:

> 'As we sat at tea, a telegraph boy cycled to the door and on opening it my father went deadly white and read the telegram from the War Office that they regretted that Lieutenant C Gold had been killed in action. My father's grief and my mother's bravery were agonising and it was some years before the blow became dulled by time. He had been such a model son, hard-working, witty, excelling not only in sports and games but also in the academic field that it was difficult to believe that this career which promised so much should be cut short. Relatives, friends, associates and fellow soldiers sent a flood of condolences and a memorial plaque was erected to him in Eton College cloisters.'

On 20 August the General Officer Commanding 12th Division

presented decorations awarded for gallantry on 3 July. (Only those marked with an asterisk were present to receive the awards):

Military Cross to
2nd Lt HM Brown (Died of wounds), 2nd Lt AD Breach.

Distinguished Conduct Medal to
Sgt HG Nicholls, Cpl CP Howard.*

Military Medal to

Sgt J Bunce	Sgt E Wardley*
Cpl WS Hammond*	Cpl W Pearmine*
Pte P Allison*	Pte J Gardner
Pte J Macfarlane	Pte A Purchell
Pte E Robbins	Pte AI Smith.*

Old German trenches
near Ovillers
(IWM Q4123)

German counter-
attacks on 8 August

After a brief period in billets the battalion started training again on 11 July, having received drafts of reinforcements. On 7 August they moved into the front line and relieved units of 36th Brigade in trenches north-west of Pozières. Throughout the relief they were subjected to heavy German shelling. Only a matter of hours after they had settled into their positions the Germans launched a series of local attacks using Flammenwerfer (flame throwers) and grenades designed to dislodge them from their position in Ration Trench.

The first two attacks came at 3.00 am the following morning. German troops assaulting on the left flank gained a footing in the trench, but they were driven out. A simultaneous attack from the right using Flammenwerfer and directed against a bombing stop or barricade which protected the flank of the battalion was repelled after hand-to-hand fighting. Another Flammenwerfer attack followed two hours later and this time the Royal Berkshires were compelled to give up their barricade and withdraw down the trench. A fresh barricade was constructed and the position was held. A final German effort at 7.30 am was easily repelled.

The net result of these actions was that the Germans gained some 50 yards of trench and both sides suffered heavy losses, the Royal Berkshires sustaining six officer casualties. Company Commander Second Lieutenant FAL Edwards who had conducted the defence with great gallantry was wounded and died two days later. His Adjutant later wrote:

'He was the bravest man in the trenches. All the men say he was simply wonderful on the morning of 8 August. We lost a very gallant soldier and a very lovable man. It may be mentioned that the enemy twice attacked under cover of liquid fire and Second Lieutenant Edwards held them off. He was badly wounded in the head while constructing a barricade within 25 yards of the enemy.'

Second Lieutenant GM Hughes was wounded in the first attack and after first being reported missing was later recorded as killed. Second Lieutenant H Crowhurst was wounded by a German grenade and Second Lieutenants HM Thurston, A Bidmead and AJ Shipton were all wounded by the shell-fire which greeted them on their arrival in Ration Trench. According to 35th Brigade returns, of the other ranks' casualties 15 were killed, 72 were wounded and 10 were reported missing.

The British Official History sums up these events in half a sentence: '...on the right the 5th Royal Berkshires were forced to retire some distance after fierce fighting in which both sides sustained heavy loss...'

Details of the Flammenwerfer operations were recorded by an officer in 36th Brigade, Captain SC Cazalet:

> 'One man creeps forward with the hose whilst another pumps up pressure in a tank to keep up the supply. As soon as the smoke appears, bombers use this as a screen and get within easy throwing distance on the flanks. Men working on the Flammenwerfer appeared to be clad in shiny black oilskins.'

Captain Cazalet's impression was that the flames were of short duration but that thick smoke hung about for some considerable time. A 12th Division Intelligence Report for 8 August estimated the range of the flame to be about 25 yards with eight jets being used at any one time. The same report added rather enigmatically: 'The enemy still walks about in small parties headed by a Red Cross flag – these were fired on and dispersed.'

On the following day further casualties were caused in Ration Trench by shell-fire: Second Lieutenant RA Bance was killed, Lieutenant C de V Hinde and Second Lieutenants AGC Rice and HC Toogood were wounded. 39 other ranks became casualties.

Military Medals for gallant conduct during the fighting on 7,8 and 9 August were awarded on 10 September to:

Sgt W Francis	Cpl HW Hestor
Cpl HJ Matthews	L/Cpl F Amor
L/Cpl G Bennett	L/Cpl GF Epsley
L/Cpl E Harwood	Pte FJ Allen
Pte TG Baker	Pte A Clarke
Pte A Dobble	Pte J Garlick (bar)
Pte LW Perris	Pte F Pike.

Following this action the 5th Battalion came out of the line and by the end of August had left the Somme area to move up to Arras. They were on the Somme again in October, mainly in reserve or support, before returning to Arras.

Battle of the Somme. A crowded road at Fricourt.

Staff-cars, mule-limbers, lorries, ambulance,
infantry marching and pioneers road widening.
13 October 1916 (IWM Q5794)

5 The 8th Battalion

The role of the 8th Battalion during the Battle of the Somme was essentially one of support in three separate engagements: on 14 July, on 18 August and on 3 September. During this period the battalion and its division were under 111 Corps which operated in the area to the south-east of the Albert-Bapaume road, taking in Contalmaison, Mametz Wood, Bazentin le Petit, Bazentin le Grand and High Wood.

Arrival on the Somme

The battalion arrived on the Somme on 9 July, marching to billets in Albert about 11.30 pm. On the following day they left Albert and took over two trenches near Lozenge Wood. Early on the morning of 11 July Second Lieutenant FS Snell was killed whilst reconnoitering from Lozenge Wood in the direction of Contalmaison. At 9.30 pm the battalion moved out of the trenches near Lozenge Wood and relieved the 8th Yorks and Lancs who had captured Contalmaison the previous night. The Royal Berkshires established themselves on the eastern edge of the village, occupying two trenches in the grounds of the chateau. The 1st Black Watch were on their left and battalion HQ was in the cellar of a ruined house just behind the chateau.

The scene in Contalmaison was described in an article published in the *Berkshire Chronicle* on 18 August 1916 and presumably submitted by a member of the battalion:

'The village had been taken a few hours previously and the battalion was to be sent in to hold it at all costs and to consolidate it, as it had already been taken and retaken three times. The battalion moved into the village and the sight that met their eyes was one which the men say they will never forget. The Germans were shelling the village of which not one house was left standing.

Three or four cellars which had been reinforced by the Germans were still intact and these the Germans were doing their best to destroy. The dead and dying of both sides were everywhere lying amongst the other debris, whilst the smell was anything but inviting. One cellar was used as a dressing station and the Medical Officer in taking over found to his surprise that the place was already occupied by a German doctor.

45

About 20 of the enemy's wounded had been there with hardly any food for 10 days during which the ownership of the village had been in some doubt. We gave them food and the German Medical Officer helped in treating our wounded. He and the German wounded were taken to the rear and sent away under escort. Little groups of Germans were turning up in all sorts of places, some showing fight, but the majority surrendering willingly.'

Preparations for the attack on 14 July

By the evening of 12 July the battalion had consolidated a line from the northern corner of the chateau grounds along a sunken road to the western edge of Mametz Wood. A bombing patrol had been sent up Pearl Alley – the main communication trench between the sunken road and the German second line defences – where a post had been established at a distance of some 300 yards. During the day the Commanding Officer, Lieutenant-Colonel TG Dalby, had been wounded whilst returning from a visit to the sunken road. At midnight Pearl Wood, lying to the north in No Man's Land, was seized and consolidated by a patrol led by Second Lieutenant FG Marsh.

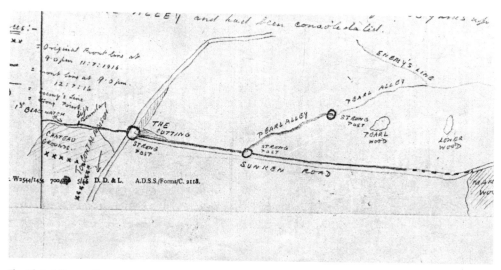

The 8th Battalion position east of Contalmaison as drawn in the battalion War Diary for July 1916

As a further preliminary to the forthcoming attack a patrol of 20 men with two Lewis Gun teams under Second Lieutenant GR Goodship was sent out on the following evening from the sunken road and they seized Lower Wood, to the right of Pearl Wood, some 350 yards ahead in No Man's Land. Goodship later gave an account of this action to the regimental historian:

'Just before dusk an urgent order was received for an officer and party to occupy Lower Wood.... The only men available were Corporal Belcher, Sergeant Woodfield and myself and others mustering 17 in all. When we arrived at the front line I issued my instructions, deployed, and was just going to advance when a terrific shelling from the enemy started, which, together with the darkness, disorganised the party.

However, with the aid of the sergeant and corporal, I got together eight or nine men, and leaving the sergeant to find the remainder, advanced in open order, under fire, across some four hundred yards of open ground and straight through the wood to the opposite side. All was well, the enemy scuttling. Leaving a sentry group of three, the remainder of us scoured the wood as best we could (we did it thoroughly at dawn) and then, to the best of our ability, consolidated the position.

The sergeant later arrived with four or five men, two being missing (afterwards found killed). At dawn one Lewis Gun and two machine-guns were sent forward. The artillery zero was 5.20 am and the infantry 9.00 am, and I have never seen land look so much like a rough sea as on that occasion. Four men were killed, four wounded and one gun completely destroyed before we were relieved at sundown. The wood seen on the morning of the 13th was beautiful and green; when we left there was scarce a branch on the trunks.'

**Pearl Alley
14 July**

On 14 July Fourth Army mounted a dawn attack on the German second position. Troops formed up in the darkness in No Man's Land to within 200 yards of the enemy lines. 21st Division on the left of the front was attacking Bazentin le Grand Wood and Bazentin le Petit Wood and village. The job of 1st Division was to form a flank on its left with an attack by the 8th Royal Berkshires up the trench known as Pearl Alley. A combined attack of the two divisions was planned for 2.30 pm but was postponed to 4.30 pm because 21st Division could not expel the enemy from the north-west corner of Bazentin le Petit Wood and was suffering from German artillery fire. At 3.00 pm a heavy German counter-attack against the village and the northern face of the wood caused the attack to be abandoned altogether.

However, acting on their orders received during the morning, the 8th Battalion were already on their way by 1.00 pm. They had set off an hour and a half early because of the condition of Pearl Alley, which was waist high in liquid mud. They reached the German trench but were driven out by a counter-attack across open ground and they retired down Pearl Alley to their original line. At 11.30 pm the battalion was relieved by the 1st Gloucesters and went back to billets in Albert.

Battalion casualties for the period 11–14 July were reported as:
Officers killed

2nd Lt FS Snell, 2nd Lt GE Maggs (died of wounds)

Shells bursting on British wire,
Bazentin le Grand, September
1916 (IWM Q4119)

Officers wounded
    Lt-Col TG Dalby, Lt HC Churchill,
    Lt ACP Lunn, 2nd Lt PGM Morris.
Other ranks
    8 killed, 123 wounded, 2 missing.

The battalion had played only a subsidiary role in the operations of 14 July but it is worth repeating that the Fourth Army attack itself was one of the clear successes of the Battle of the Somme. Surprise had been achieved and the German second position on a front of 6,000 yards had been taken, including the two Bazentins with their woods and, further to the east, part of the village of Longueval and the whole of Trones Wood.

For the remainder of July the battalion saw little front line action, being in support or reserve positions. From 25 July to 13 August they were based in Baisieux Wood where fresh drafts were received and the battalion was re-organised. Training in 'open warfare' was carried out and night assaults were practised. On 14 August the men moved into brigade reserve on the northern edge of Mametz Wood and at noon on the 18th they relieved the 1st Black Watch in the front line north of Bazentin le Petit.

Intermediate Line 18 August

As part of 111 Corps operations north of Bazentin le Petit planned for 18 August the 1st Brigade of 1st Division was to capture the remaining portion of the Intermediate Line, a German trench running east from the road leading from Bazentin le Petit to Martinpuich. Part of the Intermediate Line was already held by the 2nd Brigade. The attack was to be made by three companies of the 8th Royal Berkshires: 'D' on the right, 'B' in the centre and 'C' on the left. 'A' Company was in reserve. The 10th Gloucesters were on their right.

The bombardment began at noon. Heavy artillery shells fell in the Royal Berkshire trenches coming, it was believed, from British guns. This shelling cut communications between the companies and so demolished Lancs Trench on the left that a platoon which had been detailed to attack from this direction was unable to reach its starting point. It was decided that the parties which should have assaulted from the left should join in the frontal assault.

49

The Commanding Officer of the 8th Battalion, now Lieutenant-Colonel C Bartlett, gave the following account of the action in the battalion War Diary:

> 'At 2.45 pm the three companies did a frontal attack on the enemy's Intermediate Line. The report of the officer commanding the left company who returned wounded was to the effect that the smoke sent out by the 15th Division blew across our front so that they could not tell in which direction they were going. The remains of the company afterwards joined up with those that were left of the other two companies who had reached a shallow trench about 100 yards in front of our front line and had started to consolidate, it being impossible to progress further owing to machine-gun fire. Captain Birch was the only officer with this party and he tried to hold on to the trench with the men he had but was very heavily shelled and forced to retire to our own line again.'

Lt-Col C Bartlett

The failure of the battalion to reach their objective was due, according to Lieutenant-Colonel Bartlett, to:

- lack of time for preliminary organisation and for the troops to gain some knowledge of the ground
- the intensity of the enemy's machine-gun fire which caused many casualties, especially in the right company
- the loss of so many officers.

Battalion casualties for 18 August were:
Officers killed
    2nd Lt WN Conyers, 2nd Lt CGB Harrison,
    2nd Lt WH Bissley.
Officers wounded
    Lt SF Stileman, 2nd Lt GR Goodship, 2nd Lt SAG Harvey,
    2nd Lt DW Prout.
Other ranks: 160.
    On the following day 2nd Lt ES Joy was killed on patrol.

From 20 to 28 August the battalion was in support trenches north of Mametz Wood. From here they moved to High Wood where they relieved the 1st Cameron Highlanders. On 30 August a German attack was driven off by machine-guns from High Wood. An enemy party tried to enter a sap on the Royal Berkshire front to the west of High Wood but was repulsed. The battalion was relieved by the 2nd Royal Sussex and returned to Mametz Wood.

High Wood
3 September

Fourth Army plans for the operations on 3 September included an attack on Wood Lane Trench and the German front line at High Wood. On 2 September the battalion moved in to support the 1st Camerons. Two companies 'A' and 'B' were placed at the disposal of the Officer Commanding 1st Camerons and occupied Rifles Trench south-east of the wood.

Zero hour on 3 September was noon. The 1st Camerons attacked Wood Lane with all four companies in line and with the detachment of the Royal Berkshires alongside them. In the centre and on the left the Camerons took the trench after hand-to-hand fighting and gained another 100 yards before beginning to consolidate. At 3.00 pm the Germans counter-attacked from the Switch Line north-east of High Wood. They enfiladed the left of the Camerons who, together with the men of the Royal Berkshires, retired to their original line at about 3.30 pm. An hour later the right of the battalion also retired, having taken some 80 prisoners.

A brief report of this action appeared in the *Reading Mercury* on 4 November 1916 and in the *Berkshire Chronicle* on 17 November:

> 'It was to the right of High Wood that the battalion went over. A mine went up at noon; this was the signal to go over, the objectives being a ridge and a sunken road. Some of the Berkshires were wounded by our own barrage. The Germans had been subjected to heavy bombardment for two or three days previously and it seemed that nothing could live against it, but when the shelling ceased the enemy came out in droves for a counter-attack.'

Battalion casualties for 3 September were reported as:
Officers killed
    2nd Lt LG Edens.
Officers missing, later recorded as killed
    2nd Lt CH Chambers.
Officers wounded, missing, later recorded as killed
    2nd Lt DW Prout.
Officers wounded
    Capt JHG Lawrence, Lt G Baker, Lt SE Davenport,
    2nd Lt GF Marsh.
Other ranks: 100.

On 5 September the battalion was relieved and went into bivouac in Bécourt Wood. On 24 September they moved back to Bazentin le Grand from where they were relieved and moved out of the line for the remainder of the month to Bresle.

1st Brigade spent the month of October in training. The 8th Royal Berkshires were afflicted with, of all things, an epidemic of German measles, and had to remain behind when the rest of the brigade departed. They finally arrived in Albert on 27 November, after the close of the Somme campaign. For the remainder of 1916 they were located near the two Bazentins, spending Christmas Day in the front-line trenches and New Year's Eve back in billets in Albert.

Destroyed German trenches
at Ovillers (IWM Q4044)

6 After the battle: the old German line

'We amused ourselves by strolling round the old German trenches where our men had fought weeks before and I don't think I shall ever forget those few days. We went up those old trenches which were littered with broken rifles, parts of equipment, tunics, great-coats, both ours and German, ammunition, tins of bully beef, steel helmets, shell cases and many other things. The worst things we saw were mounds and little wooden crosses, several of them having on them the words: "Here lies the body of an unknown British soldier". He would probably be reported missing and his friends still wondering if he was still alive.

Shell holes were all over the place large and small, also dud shells with their noses buried in the ground. German bombs were lying about as well as some of our Mills bombs. In some parts lay the remains of one of our guns or transport wagons that had been hit by a shell and nearby were the graves of those who belonged to the guns or of the drivers of the wagon. Barbed wire lay everywhere, having been blown to pieces by our artillery. There were also large piles of boxes that had contained shells and these we made free use of for firewood and improving our bivouacs.'

The Somme battlefield in October 1916 as described in his diary by SP Ambrose. Private Ambrose enlisted in Reading on 10 November 1914 and after service with the 2/4th Battalion was transferred to the 5th Battalion in 1916.

Royal Berkshire Regiment
Western Front Service Battalions: fatal casualties during the Somme campaign

July

	5th Btn	6th Btn	8th Btn	Total
1	**0**	**92**	**0**	**92**
2	1	8	1	10
3	**96**	**0**	**0**	**96**
4	0	0	0	0
5	0	1	0	1
6	0	0	0	0
7	0	1	0	1
8	1	0	0	1
9	1	1	0	2
10	0	1	0	1
11	0	1	1	2
12	0	1	4	5
13	2	1	5	8
14	**0**	**2**	**13**	**15**
15	0	0	0	0
16	0	0	0	0
17	0	1	0	1
18	0	2	1	3
19	**4**	**36**	**1**	**41**
20	0	3	0	3
21	0	2	0	2
22	0	1	3	4
23	0	2	2	4
24	0	0	5	5
25	0	1	6	7
26	1	1	1	3
27	0	2	0	2
28	1	0	1	2
29	0	0	0	0
30	6	0	0	6
31	0	0	0	0
Totals	113	160	44	317

August

	5th Btn	6th Btn	8th Btn	Total
1	0	0	0	0
2	0	0	0	0
3	0	0	0	0
4	0	0	0	0
5	0	0	0	0
6	1	1	0	2
7	0	0	0	0
8	**20**	**0**	**0**	**20**
9	10	0	0	10
10	1	0	0	1
11	1	1	0	2
12	0	0	0	0
13	0	0	2	2
14	1	0	0	1
15	0	0	0	0
16	1	0	0	1
17	0	1	2	3
18	**2**	**0**	**33**	**35**
19	0	0	7	7
20	1	0	2	3
21	0	0	2	2
22	0	0	2	2
23	0	0	0	0
24	0	0	2	2
25	1	0	0	1
26	2	0	0	2
27	0	0	2	2
28	2	0	3	5
29	0	0	1	1
30	0	0	2	2
31	0	0	4	4
Totals	43	3	64	110

September

	5th Btn	6th Btn	8th Btn	Total
1	0	0	4	4
2	0	0	1	1
3	**0**	**0**	**36**	**36**
4	0	0	0	0
5	0	0	1	1
6	0	1	1	2
7	0	0	1	1
8	0	0	0	0
9	0	0	0	0
10	0	0	0	0
11	0	0	0	0
12	0	0	1	1
13	0	0	0	0
14	0	1	0	1
15	0	0	0	0
16	0	0	0	0
17	0	0	0	0
18	0	0	0	0
19	0	0	1	1
20	0	0	0	0
21	0	0	2	2
22	0	0	4	4
23	0	0	3	3
24	0	0	2	2
25	0	0	2	2
26	1	0	3	4
27	0	2	1	3
28	0	2	1	3
29	**0**	**14**	**0**	**14**
30	**0**	**12**	**0**	**12**
Totals	1	32	64	97

October

	5th Btn	6th Btn	8th Btn	Total
1	0	6	0	6
2	0	10	0	10
3	0	6	0	6
4	1	1	0	2
5	0	7	0	7
6	0	0	0	0
7	0	1	0	1
8	0	1	0	1
9	2	0	0	2
10	1	3	0	4
11	0	0	0	0
12	1	0	0	1
13	1	0	0	1
14	6	0	0	6
15	4	3	0	7
16	1	1	0	2
17	0	5	0	5
18	4	0	0	4
19	**10**	**4**	**1**	**15**
20	1	1	0	2
21	0	2	0	2
22	1	0	0	1
23	0	0	1	1
24	1	1	0	2
25	1	0	0	1
26	0	1	0	1
27	0	0	0	0
28	0	0	0	0
29	0	0	0	0
30	0	1	0	1
31	0	1	0	1
Totals	35	55	2	92

November

	5th Btn	6th Btn	8th Btn	Total
1	1	1	0	2
2	0	0	0	0
3	0	0	0	0
4	0	0	0	0
5	0	0	0	0
6	1	0	0	1
7	0	0	0	0
8	0	0	0	0
9	0	0	0	0
10	0	0	0	0
11	0	1	0	1
12	0	4	0	4
13	0	0	0	0
Totals	2	6	0	8

	5th Btn	6th Btn	8th Btn	Total
1/1/1916 – 30/6/1916	59	33	62	154
1/7/1916 – 13/11/1916	194	256	174	624
13/11/1916 – 31/12/1916	13	1	26	40
Total 1916	266	290	262	818

Days with more than
10 fatalities are in bold

7 The cost of 1916

Given the tenacity of the German defenders on the Somme, the strength of their positions and the technical limitations – above all in communications and artillery – to which the attacking armies were subject, it is not surprising that territorial gains were limited and casualties shockingly heavy. This is true of many of the actions in which the Royal Berkshire battalions were engaged and in bringing their story to a close it is perhaps fitting to remember those who gave their lives during the campaign. Personal details of the fatal casualties and their commemoration are given in Appendix III but the bare statistics of the losses can also tell us something, as the accompanying table shows.

The varying success of the three battalions during the campaign and the different levels of their involvement in front-line action throughout the whole of 1916 have been major themes of the preceding narrative. Yet what is striking about the summary totals of fatal casualties for the year is how similar these are. One explanation is perhaps that the daily wear and tear of trench warfare – both in the line and out – was over a long period a levelling factor.

Also striking is the inference, at least from this evidence, that success or failure in attack did not make a significant difference to the casualty rates. The 6th Battalion's success at Montauban on 1 July and the 5th Battalion's failure at Ovillers on 3 July produced almost identical losses – 92 in the one, 96 in the other. Each day caused about one third of the battalion's fatal casualties for the whole of the year. Perhaps again the explanation here is the very nature of warfare on the Western Front once the trench system had developed. Despite an increasing sophistication in the use of artillery and the deployment of tanks in growing numbers, the successes achieved in the later years still had to be bought at the expense of infantrymen's lives. There were no cheap short cuts to victory.

The local costs of these two attacks are also worth remembering. Of the 6th Battalion's dead on 1 July, 21 came from Berkshire; of the 5th Battalion's on 3 July, 33 were Berkshiremen. Almost half of the 5th Battalion's fatal casualties on that day were men who had come over together in May 1915 and had shared the experience of the Battle of Loos.

Another more general aspect of the war on the Western Front made graphically obvious in the table is the relative infrequency of a battalion's involvement in full-scale actions. Out of some 136 days of campaigning on the Somme, only ten days produced joint fatal casualties for the three battalions of more than ten. For the individual infantryman – even during a major campaign – waiting was a more prominent feature of life than fighting.

The result of the losses presented here – and of the numbers of men who were wounded and out of action for shorter or longer periods – was that the composition of the three Royal Berkshire battalions had changed dramatically by the end of 1916. Figures have already been given to illustrate the effects of reinforcement as far as the 6th Battalion is concerned. The 5th and 8th Battalions had already undergone a similar process of renewal during and after the Battle of Loos in 1915. The campaigns of the last two years of the war were going to be fought by battalions which bore little resemblance to those first formed in the autumn of 1914.

8 The Somme: a postscript

In terms of territorial objectives, the Battle of the Somme brought about a maximum British advance of 10 miles. In human terms the British (and Empire) forces suffered in round figures 420,000 casualties, the French 195,000, the Germans – at their own estimation – 500,000. More significant than the ground gained by fighting was that abandoned by the German army early in 1917 when it retired to the prepared positions of the Siegfried Stellung – or Hindenburg Line as it was known to the British. The exhausting effects of the five-month campaign on the German army – coupled with its contribution to the survival of Verdun – might well be considered in the longer perspective to be its most significant aspect. Worth recalling is the letter General Rawlinson received from GHQ on 16 June 1916 telling him that his Fourth Army was undertaking offensive operations 'with the object of relieving the pressure on the French at Verdun and inflicting loss on the enemy.'

The Battle of the Somme is today remembered for its scale, its length, the number of casualties suffered on the first day, especially in the Kitchener divisions, and for the type of warfare – 'attrition' – into which it seemed to degenerate. It has furnished many of the stereotypes of the Western Front which frequently reappear in television documentaries and popular journalism: mud and horror, uncaring and incompetent staff officers sending brave men to their certain deaths against uncut wire and German machine-guns. Like all stereotypes these reflect a certain reality of experience; at the same time they block a more differentiated analysis which could accommodate success as well as failure, which could see the Battle of the Somme not as a static example of 'futility' but as an early – and very costly – struggle to come to terms with the technological demands of a twentieth-century form of siege warfare from which lessons could and would be learned.

Sources
Unpublished

Public Record Office, Kew	War Diaries (WO95)
	   431 Fourth Army
	   895 XIII Corps
	   1231 1st Division
	   1261 1st Brigade
	   1265 8th Battalion, Royal Berkshire Regiment
	   1735 9th Division
	   1823 12th Division
	   1847 35th Brigade
	   1850 5th Battalion, Royal Berkshire Regiment
	   2015 18th Division
	   2034 53rd Brigade
	   2037 6th Battalion, Royal Berkshire Regiment
	   2040 8th Battalion, Norfolk Regiment
	   2046 55th Brigade
	
	Correspondence between GHQ and Army HQs
	(WO158/234)
	
	Official War Histories: Correspondence and Papers
	(CAB45/132-138)

Imperial War Museum, London	Papers of General Sir Ivor Maxse KCB CVO DSO (69/53/7 69/53/8) Papers of H Harding, F Henwood, AJ Gosling and TA Jennings, 6th Battalion, Royal Berkshire Regiment
The Royal Gloucestershire, Berkshire and Wiltshire Regiment (Salisbury) Museum	War Diaries 5th, 6th and 8th Battalions, Royal Berkshire Regiment

In private hands	The Great War Letters from Cecil, Pat and Alec Gold
	   (5th Battalion, Royal Berkshire Regiment)
	   Vol 3 January – September 1916 (Gold family)
	Papers of SP Ambrose (PA Watkins)
	Papers of Harold Ackroyd (EF Malet de Carteret)
	Papers of Patrick Gold (Gold family)

Published

Official publications

War Office, *Officers Died in the Great War 1914–1919*
    (n.e. Polstead 1988)
War Office, *Soldiers Died in the Great War 1914–1919* Pt 52
    (n.e. Polstead 1989)
Edmonds, J.E., *Military Operations France & Belgium, 1916*
    Vol. 1 (London 1932)
    Appendices (London 1932)
Miles, W., *Military Operations France & Belgium, 1916*
    Vol. 2 (London 1938)

Newspapers and journals

Berkshire Chronicle
Maidenhead Advertiser
Newbury Weekly News
Reading Mercury
Reading Standard
Berkshire and the War:
    The *Reading Standard* Pictorial Record,
    (Reading 1916–1919)
China Dragon: The Journal of the Royal Berkshire Regiment,
    (Princess Charlotte of Wales's), 1914–1959
The Journal of the Duke of Edinburgh's Royal Regiment,
    (Berkshire and Wiltshire), 1959–1994

Other works

Falls, C., *The First World War* (London 1960)
Hurst, S.C., *The Silent Cities: An Illustrated Guide to the War
    Cemeteries and Memorials to the 'Missing' in France and
    Flanders 1914–1918* (London 1929)
Middlebrook, M.& M., *The Somme Battlefields* (London 1994)
Nichols, G.H.F., *The 18th Division in the Great War* (London 1922)
Petre, F. Loraine., *The Royal Berkshire Regiment* (Reading 1925)
Prior, R. & Wilson, T., *Command on the Western Front* (Oxford 1992)
Scott, A.B. & Brumwell, P.M., *History of the 12th (Eastern) Division in
    the Great War* (London 1923)
Simpson, A., *The Evolution of Victory* (London 1995)
Terraine, J., *Haig: The Educated Soldier* (London 1990)

Appendix I

Thirty men: brief biographies of some of those who served with the battalions in 1916

The 5th Battalion

Sergeant
George Bennett MM & Bar

Sergeant Bennett lived at Laurel Cottage, Murrell Green, King's St., Wokingham. At the outbreak of war, aged 21, he enlisted as a Kitchener volunteer and was posted to the 5th Battalion. He went with the battalion to France on 30 May 1915. He was promoted to sergeant and awarded the Military Medal for gallant conduct on 7, 8 and 9 August 1916, when the Germans made four counter-attacks on the battalion positions in Ration Trench north-west of Pozières. He was wounded on at least two occasions and spent some time sick in hospital in October 1916. He was awarded a Bar to his Military Medal for operations during the latter half of October 1918. He survived the remainder of the war, being demobilised on 13 March 1919.

Second Lieutenant
AD Breach MC

Second Lieutenant Breach was employed at Huntley & Palmers, Reading, before the war. Together with a colleague, Cyril Thorne, he joined the Hampshire Regiment and they became almost inseparable. They both performed similar duties in the Hampshire Regiment, received their 'stripes' together and on the same day as each other they were granted their commissions. 2nd Lt Breach joined the 5th Battalion of the Royal Berkshire Regiment on 5 June 1916, 2nd Lt Thorne being posted to the 8th Battalion. On 3 July 1916 the 5th Battalion made an unsuccessful and costly attack on the German positions at Ovillers. The battalion War Diary states:

> '...at 4.00 pm the battalion which consisted of 70 men and the Colonel were withdrawn to the Albert defences...in the evening 2nd Lts

Breach and May plus 60 men, who had dug in, in No Man's Land, joined them.'

On 20 August 1916 the General Officer Commanding 12th Division presented decorations for operations on 3 July. 2nd Lt Breach, who was sick in England, was unable to be present to receive his Military Cross. The *London Gazette* citation dated August 1916 reads:

> 'For conspicuous gallantry in action. He led his platoon against the enemy trenches with great dash. Later, when entrenching a position, he set a fine example to his men by personal coolness.'

Second Lieutenant Harold Masters Brown MC

Second Lieutenant Brown, third son of Mr & Mrs C Brown, Slinfold, Sussex, was educated at Horsham Grammar School and King's College, London, where he was awarded a BSc Hons Degree. Before the war he was a science master at King's School Canterbury. At the outbreak of war he and his younger brother joined the Coldstream Guards. In March 1915 he gained a commission in the 9th Battalion of the Royal Berkshire Regiment and was trained at Sevenoaks, Portsmouth and Wool. He went to France in October 1915 and was attached to the 5th Battalion of the Royal Berkshire Regiment. Owing to his unfailing interest in his men, he was known to officers and men as Father Brown.

On 3 July 1916 during the battalion attack on Ovillers, he was in charge of 'C' Company. He crossed the German first line of

trenches but was then wounded by a bomb in the arms, legs and abdomen. The man who carried him out of the trenches, Lance-Corporal Charles Woodley of Reading, was himself shot and killed. About an hour later 2nd Lt Brown was picked up and taken to the Duchess of Westminster Red Cross Hospital. His elder brother, on learning of his being wounded, immediately set off for France and arrived in time to hear an account of the action. On Sunday 9 July 2nd Lt Brown died, aged 28, in his brother's arms. He is buried in Etaples Military Cemetery. He was posthumously awarded the Military Cross for his conduct during the actions on 3 July 1916.

The *London Gazette* citation dated August 1916 reads:

> 'For conspicuous gallantry in action, on several occasions, notably when he carried out a dangerous reconnaissance of the enemy trenches and afterwards led his company to the attack with great dash. He was wounded in five places.'

Lance-Corporal Joseph H Bunce MM

Lance-Corporal Bunce, who lived in Hitchen near Maidenhead, went to France with the 2nd Battalion of the Royal Berkshire Regiment and was later transferred to the 5th Battalion. He was promoted to sergeant and was awarded the Military Medal for operations on 3 July 1916. L/Cpl Bunce was with the party under 2nd Lt AD Breach when his platoon got into the second line of the German trenches and later dug themselves in in No Man's Land. His Military Medal was awarded for general good work and for bravery. Whilst dug in he frequently carried messages back to the British lines under heavy fire. He also rendered great assistance in bringing in the wounded. At the end of the war he had reached the rank of company sergeant-major.

Second Lieutenant Howard Mortimer Cook

Second Lieutenant Cook, born 1 September 1889, was the elder son of Mr John R Cook who lived at 1 Erleigh Road, Reading. He was the grandson of Mr Day, formerly Town Clerk of Reading. He was educated at Reading School and St Edmund Hall, Oxford, where he rowed in the College Eight. At the outbreak of the war he was on the point of leaving for Holland to take up a teaching post. He applied for a commission at once and in the meantime joined a Public Schools battalion as a private. In November 1914 he was gazetted to the 6th Battalion of the Royal Berkshire Regiment. 2nd Lt Cook went to France in February 1916, having been attached to the 5th Battalion. On 13 April

1916 he was wounded in the head by shrapnel and was moved to hospital in Torquay. After a few months at home he returned to the front where he served as Company Commander on the Somme. In 1917 he distinguished himself at the Battle of Cambrai and in February 1918 was sent to England for transfer to the Machine Gun Corps. On 9 August 1918, aged 30, he was killed by the explosion of a mine when taking his section into action at night. He is buried in Contay British Cemetery.

Second Lieutenant Francis Andrew Lloyd Edwards MC

Second Lieutenant Edwards was the youngest son of Captain HH Edwards RN and Mrs Edwards of Broadlands Cholsey, and was educated at Reading School and at the City and Guilds College, Kensington. He joined the army at the outbreak of war and was commissioned in November 1914 into the Devon Fortress Engineers. In 1915 he was transferred to the 5th Battalion of the Royal Berkshire Regiment. On the morning of 8 August 1916 the Germans made four counter-attacks on the battalion positions near Pozières and forced the Royal Berkshires to withdraw down their trench. Whilst supervising the construction of a barricade 2nd Lt Edwards, who had conducted the defence with great gallantry, was badly wounded in the head. He died of his wounds on 10 August 1916 and was buried in Puchevillers British Cemetery. He was awarded the Military Cross for these actions and the *London Gazette* citation dated 26 September 1916 reads:

> 'For conspicuous gallantry during operations. When the enemy twice attacked under cover of liquid fire, 2nd Lt Edwards showed great pluck under most trying circumstances and held off the enemy. He was badly wounded in the head while constructing a barricade within 25 yards of the enemy.'

Lieutenant
Cecil Argo Gold

Lieutenant Gold was the eldest son of Argo and Mary Gold of Bray Lawn, Bray, Berkshire and 31 Gloucester Square, London. His two younger brothers also served as officers in the 5th Battalion of the Royal Berkshire Regiment. He was educated at Evelyn's Prep School, Austin Leigh's House, Eton College and Magdalen College, Oxford. On leaving Oxford he joined a well known firm of solicitors. After the outbreak of war he volunteered for service with the Royal Berkshire Regiment, was posted to the 5th Battalion on 24 November 1914 and was appointed Adjutant on 14 October 1915. He was mentioned in Sir Douglas Haig's Dispatches on 30 April

1916. On 3 July 1916, during the attack on Ovillers, the Battalion Commander Lt-Col Willan, together with Lt Gold, went forward to the German trenches and, recognising that the attack had stalled and that there was no cover, withdrew what men he could collect and made them dig in on the Albert-Ovillers sunken road. It was whilst supervising this work that Lt Gold was struck in the head by a bullet and killed. His body was later brought in by Captain RH Causton. Lt Gold is buried in Aveluy Communal Cemetery Extension and he is commemorated by a family plaque in the cloisters of Eton College.

Private
Harry Harding

Private Harding, of 10 Adelaide Road, Reading, was an improver at the Eastern Press, Reading when war broke out. He immediately enlisted at the Royal Berkshire Regiment Depot, Brock Barracks, and following several months training at Shorncliffe, near Folkestone, he went with the 5th Battalion to France on 31 May 1915. Having served with the 5th Battalion throughout the war he volunteered to remain with the cadre of 4 officers and 38 men which stayed on after the troops had returned home. The cadre, which included 16 'originals' who had served with the battalion throughout the war, returned to a civic reception in Reading on 18 June 1919. In September 1980 Mr Harding, now living at 23 St Peter's Road, Earley, Reading, published a record of his war service with the 5th Battalion, entitled 'From the City and the Plough'. A copy is deposited with the Imperial War Museum and may be consulted there.

Captain
Joe Conquest James

Captain James, son of Mr WJ James, was educated at Cranleigh and Reading School. On leaving school he went to South Africa and joined the British South African Police. During the South African War he

served as a trooper in Thorneycroft's Mounted Infantry and received the Queen's & King's Medals, with four clasps. After the war he became the proprietor of the Wellington Hotel, Wellington College Station. In September 1914 he joined the Berkshire Royal Horse Artillery as a gun-

ner and in December 1914 he received a captaincy with the Royal Berkshire Regiment. He went to France with the 5th Battalion in May 1915. He was wounded by a shell whilst leading his company in the attack at Ovillers on 3 July 1916, was taken to hospital in Boulogne and died after an operation on 14 July 1916, at the age of 40. His wife arrived too late to see him before he died. He is buried in Wimereux Communal Cemetery.

Captain
Percival Backwith Wace

Captain Wace who attended Trinity College, Oxford, went to France with the 5th Battalion of the Royal Berkshire Regiment in 1915. He was wounded by a shell-burst on 11 July 1915. He was killed in action on 3 July 1916 during the attack on Ovillers. The battalion diarist recorded the circumstances:

> 'The bulk of the men fell back to the German Front Line trench. Some were inclined to go further, others stood at the top and appeared not to know what to do. Captain Wace was attempting to rally men and get them to go forward...'

Captain Wace was mentioned in dispatches for these actions and his name is recorded on the Thiepval Memorial to the Missing.

6th Battalion

Company Sergeant-Major Henry James Bartholomew DCM

Company Sergeant-Major Bartholomew was born at Great Bedwyn, Wiltshire, and lived at Newtown, Shellbourne, Hungerford. Before the war he was Town Sergeant in the service of the Southampton Corporation and before that was a member of the Southampton Police Force. He went to France with the 6th Battalion of the Royal Berkshire Regiment on 25 July 1915. He was mentioned in dispatches and was awarded the Distinguished Conduct Medal for his conduct during the Battle of the Somme in July 1916. The *London Gazette* citation dated 20 October 1916 reads:

> 'For conspicuous gallantry during operations in which he organised and maintained a constant supply of bombs and ammunition and, on so many occasions, went fearlessly through the enemy's heavy barrage entirely indifferent to personal danger.'

On 8 May 1917, at the age of 37, CSM (now Regimental Sergeant-Major) Bartholomew was killed by a shell, together with Privates AW Allen, J Razey and A Stone, whilst standing near a dug-out on the Arras battlefield. They are buried together in London Cemetery, Neuville Vitasse.

Second Lieutenant Godfrey Mitchell Courage

Second Lieutenant Courage was educated at Cheam, Osborne and Dartmouth Colleges and served as a midshipman on HMS Dominion. He left the navy at his own request. At the outbreak of war he volunteered for the army and was posted to the 6th Battalion of the Royal Berkshire Regiment in October 1914. He was mentioned in dispatches on 15 June 1916.

At 7.50 am on 1 July 1916, 2nd Lt Courage was sent to take command of 'B' Company, the left leading company of the first wave in the attack on Pommiers Trench. This company had suffered heavy casualties and had no officers remaining. 2nd Lt Courage too was killed, aged 20, and he is buried in Carnoy Military Cemetery.

Lieutenant, Acting Captain
George Cyril Freeman

Lieutenant Freeman was the eldest son of George Freeman JP and Mrs Freeman of 'Picketts', Horley. He was educated at Tonbridge School and Gonville and Caius College, Cambridge, where he took his degree in December 1913. He was a good shot and was captain of the Tonbridge School Eight for two years, during which time they won the Europa Cup. He gained his commission in the 5th Battalion of the Royal Berkshire Regiment in September 1915. He later transferred to the 6th Battalion and went with them to France in July 1915. He was killed in action whilst in the front line trenches at Thiepval on 1 October 1916, aged 25. He is buried in Blighty Valley Cemetery.

Private
Harold Sidney Freeman

Private Freeman was the second son of Mr Reuben Freeman of Brent Knoll, Queen's Road, Newbury. He was educated at the Boys' British School and completed his apprenticeship as a pattern maker with the Eagle Ironworks. He was a committee member of the Greenham Football Club. He enlisted in the Royal Berkshire Regiment in August 1914 and went to France

with the 6th Battalion on 25 July 1915.

Pte Freeman was wounded on the opening day of the Battle of the Somme whilst acting as a signaller. When reporting to his captain on his return from forward duty, he was told: 'You have done well, my boy, get back into the trench, slippy, or they will have you'. He was dropping into cover when a machine gun bullet struck him in the shoulder, piercing his lung. He was brought to England and treated in the Metropolitan Military Hospital at Kingsland Road but died of his wounds, aged 26, on 6 September 1916. He was buried with full military honours in Newbury Cemetery.

Second Lieutenant
Hugh Reginald Freston

Second Lieutenant 'Rex' Freston was the only son of Reginald Henry Bretingham and Elizabeth Mathilda Freston of St Catherine's Cottage, Clewer, Windsor. He was born in 1891 and was educated at Dulwich College and Exeter College, Oxford, where he read English. He joined the Officers Training Corps whilst at Oxford and was commissioned in the 3rd Battalion of the Royal Berkshires in April 1915. He was then attached to the 6th Battalion, joining them near Albert in December. During the war he had two volumes of poetry published.

At 2.00 pm on 24 January 1916, whilst in the trenches at La Boisselle, 2nd Lt Freston was killed by a trench mortar bomb. He was buried in the grounds of Bécourt Chateau but his grave is now in Bécourt Military Cemetery.

Second Lieutenant
Cyril John Fuller

Second Lieutenant Fuller was the elder son of Mr & Mrs John H Fuller, 36 Eastern Avenue, Reading. Before the war he worked in his father's business, John H Fuller Ltd, Oil and Colour Merchants of Minster Street, Reading. He went to Reading School and was a prominent member of the Reading Rowing Club and the Motor Cycle Club. He was with the Berkshire Yeomanry when the war started, but was transferred to the Royal Berkshire Regiment and gained his commission in January 1915. He was engaged in bombing and other training at Bovington, Salisbury and Colchester and went to France in March 1916. He died of wounds, aged 20, on 22 July 1916.

On his death, his captain wrote to his parents:
'...he has been through all the fighting since 1 July and his behaviour has been splendid. He and another subaltern had worked all night, under very trying conditions, the night on which he received his wounds. The next

morning the brigadier sent round to thank those two platoons for the good work done. He stayed with the battalion till the 19th, when it was too painful for him to march, and was sent to hospital.'

2nd Lt Fuller is buried in Dive Copse British Cemetery.

Private
Albert James Gosling

Private Gosling enlisted in the Royal Berkshire Regiment at Abingdon on 21 December 1914 and reported to Reading Barracks on 28 December. On 4 January 1915 he was drafted to Colchester to join the 6th Battalion. After one month of squad drill followed by full training, he passed out as 1st Class Private, and was paid three shillings and six pence per week. He applied for, and was appointed battalion bootmaker: 'more money and fewer parades' was the attraction. On 30 April 1915 he went with the battalion to Salisbury Plain and finally to Codford St Mary. The battalion was inspected near Stonehenge by H.M. The King and a few days later the men were given four days' embarkation leave before going to France on 25 July 1915.

On 1 July 1916 Pte Gosling was a member of a carrying party, a duty he was to perform at Thiepval in September and again in 1917 at Arras and Ypres. On 6 February 1918, when the battalion was disbanded, he was transferred to the 18th Entrenching Battalion. He was demobilised on 12 February 1919. He later deposited an account of his experiences with the Imperial War Museum.

Sergeant
John William Lambourne MM

Sergeant Lambourne, of 35 Leopold Road, Reading, was born at 7 Leopold Road, where his parents were still living in 1916. Before the war he worked for Huntley & Palmers. A member of the Territorials for some years, he volunteered for service overseas, and went to the front with the 6th Battalion of the Royal Berkshire Regiment early in 1916. He was wounded in the neck during the attack on Montauban Alley on 1 July 1916. In the *Berkshire Chronicle* of 8 December 1916 it was reported that he had been awarded the Military Medal:

> 'for great bravery in successfully helping to evacuate the wounded, for showing devotion to duty by taking control of the platoon after the officer had been killed and also whilst under heavy fire, taking, from the pocket of the officer, valuable papers which might have been of use to the enemy'.

(No date is given for this action but from the description it was probably whilst the battalion was at Thiepval in late September or early October 1916).

Second Lieutenant
Robert John Farquharson Remnant

Second Lieutenant Remnant, born in 1896, was the eldest son of Major JF Remnant M.P. of the Grange, Hare Hatch, Twyford. Educated at Eton, he left in August 1914 and joined the 6th Battalion of the Royal Berkshire Regiment. He went to France with the battalion on 25 July 1915 and on 16 September was invalided home with dysentery. Having recovered he was employed in England as a bombing instructor before rejoining his battalion on 24 January 1916. He was wounded on 4 March 1916 and again on 30 June 1916 at Montauban. A report in the *Berkshire Chronicle* which appeared on 21 July 1916 stated that:

> 'He was within two yards of a bomb which exploded and he was peppered all over. We understand that he was the first officer of his battalion to fall.'

When he recovered from this wound 2nd Lt Remnant joined the 4th Battalion of the Wiltshire Regiment in Palestine, where he was wounded for the third time. After the end of the war he remained in the reserve and rejoined in 1939, serving on the staff in North Africa, France and Germany. He died on 4 June 1967 at Bear Place, Twyford, Berkshire.

Lieutenant
Kenneth Robert Traill

Lieutenant Traill, youngest son of Dr & Mrs Traill of Coralee, Sunningdale, was educated at Bradfield College and London University. He entered Guy's Hospital as a medical student in 1911. He joined the Inns of Court Officers Training Corps at the outbreak of the war and received a commission in the 6th Battalion of the Royal Berkshire Regiment in September 1914, being promoted lieutenant in December 1914. He was wounded on 26 February 1916, rejoining the battalion in March. He took part in the battalion attack on Pommiers Trench on 1 July 1916. At 7.50 am it was reported that he had been killed. He is buried in Carnoy Military Cemetery.

The 8th Battalion

Second Lieutenant William Howe Bissley

Second Lieutenant Bissley was the fourth son of Mr & Mrs Frank Bissley of All Saints Avenue, Maidenhead and the husband of Mrs Ethel Muriel Bissley. He attended Maidenhead Art School and St Mark's College, Chelsea, and at the outbreak of war he was about to sit final examinations for the degree of BSc (London). For many years he was a member of the choir at All Saints Church, Boyn Hill and a teacher at the Sunday School. He was also a member of the Boyn Hill Cricket Club and the Maidenhead Hockey Club. He taught at the Essedine School, Paddington.

On the outbreak of war 2nd Lt Bissley joined the London University Officers Training Corps and in March 1915 he gained a commission in the Royal Berkshire Regiment. He went to France with the 8th Battalion in August 1915 and was made Brigade Bombing Officer. He was killed on 18 August 1916 during the unsuccessful attack north of Bazentin le Petit. He left a widow and a baby daughter. His name is recorded on the Thiepval Memorial to the Missing and also on the family grave at All Saints Churchyard, Maidenhead.

Lance-Corporal Ernest George Cole

Lance-Corporal Cole, son of Mr & Mrs James Cole of the Falcon Inn, Theale, spent most of his boyhood in Headley, where he went to school. He left a good situation in Bournemouth and was amongst the first to volunteer under the Kitchener scheme. He went to France with the 8th Battalion of the Royal Berkshire Regiment in August 1915 and was killed on 1 July 1916, aged 22, whilst acting as stretcher bearer for the 6th Battalion. The *Newbury Weekly News* of 20 July 1916 published a tribute from an RAMC captain: 'He was simply splendid, fearing nothing, so long as he could get to his wounded comrades'. His name is recorded on the Thiepval Memorial to the Missing.

Sergeant
Walter George Folley

Sergeant Folley, second son of Mr & Mrs
Folley of Park Street, Maidenhead, went to
France as a private with the 8th Battalion
of the Royal Berkshire Regiment on 7
August 1915. He was a member of the
machine gun section. He was killed by
shell-fire, aged 22, on 1 September 1916 at
a time when the battalion was out of the
line in support. Shortly before he was
killed he had to be dug out, with his uncle,
from a huge hole in which they had been
buried by a shell. Initially he was buried in
Mametz Wood, his grave being marked by
a small cross with his name painted on
it. His grave is now in Flatiron Copse
Cemetery.

Lieutenant
Gilbert Reginald Goodship

Lieutenant Goodship, who was married,
was the only son of Mr & Mrs Walter
Henry Goodship of 150 Southampton
Street, Reading. Before the war he was
with Messrs Callas Sons & May for 11
years. He was associated with St Giles
Church, where his father was verger, and
was captain of St Giles Church Lads
Brigade and a bell ringer. For some years
before the war he was a member of the
Territorials and had previously served
with the Old Volunteers.

When the war broke out Lt Goodship
joined up in the Berkshire Yeomanry,
attaining the rank of sergeant. In May
1915 he gained his commission in the
Royal Berkshire Regiment and was posted
to the 8th Battalion in France on 27 June
1916. On 18 August he was badly wounded
during an unsuccessful attack north of
Bazentin le Petit. He was hit in the chest
by a bullet which fortunately did not
touch the lung, but coming out cut the
flesh in his right arm. He was in hospital

for six months, returning to the battalion on 19 April 1917. He was promoted to the rank of lieutenant on 2 October 1917. He was reported missing on 21 March 1918 but was subsequently discovered to be a prisoner of war.

Second Lieutenant Louis Arthur Klementaski

Second Lieutenant Klementaski, eldest son of Mr SM Klementaski of 7 Tansa Road, Hampstead, was commissioned into the Royal Berkshire Regiment on 19 November 1914. He joined the 8th Battalion on 13 October 1915. On 27 May 1916 he was in charge of a wiring party in front of the British lines at Calonne when they were attacked by a large German raiding party. During the attack he was mortally wounded. According to the *Berkshire Chronicle* of 18 August 1916 a fellow officer wrote:

'It is typical of him that he should have made the stand he did, against impossible odds, and that if any of his party were to be cut off he should be with them. The German who bayoneted him was shot'.

Corporal P Holmes, a native of Skipton, was a member of the wiring party and he stayed with 2nd Lt Klementaski after the latter was wounded. He subsequently brought in his officer's body and twice went out for others. For this he was awarded the Military Medal. Cpl Holmes' mother later received from the officer's widow a watch inscribed:

'LA Klemantaski, Second Lieutenant Royal Berkshire Regiment, May 27th 1916, to Corporal P Holmes in grateful recognition of a brave deed.'

Two other members of the wiring party, Private DW Charley and Lance-Corporal GC Rowland, were also awarded the Military Medal for their bravery in helping to repel the enemy attack. Both men were later killed in action: Pte Charley on 13 July 1916 and L/Cpl Rowland on 23 June 1918.

Pte Charley is commemorated on the Thiepval Memorial to the Missing.

2nd Lt Klementaski, who was mentioned in dispatches, is buried in the Bully Grenay Communal Cemetery, British Extension.

Lance-Corporal Frank Langley

Lance-Corporal Langley, of 65 Cambridge Road, Marlow, was the son of Mr H Langley, foreman of the Marlow Urban Council. He was employed by the Buckinghamshire County Council on the district roads until he enlisted in May 1915. He

joined the 8th Battalion of the Royal Berkshire Regiment in France in December 1915. He was badly wounded in the abdomen during the attack north of Bazentin le Petit on 18 August 1916 and was admitted to 36 Casualty Clearing Station where he was operated on. His internal injuries were severe and he died on 20 August 1916 at the age of 28. He left a widow and three children under four years of age. He is buried in Heilly Station Cemetery.

Private
Harry Parsons

Private Parsons was a native of Reading and lived at 14 Caernarvon Road. He worked for Mr George Aplin, butcher of 108 King's Road, for eight years and played in the Reading Wednesday Football League. He enlisted early in 1916 and died of wounds on 25 July 1916. A Private Arthur Parsons (possibly Harry's brother) wrote to his parents from Netley Hospital, where he was being treated for shell shock

which had caused him to become deaf and dumb:

> 'The shell that caught me on 30 July 1916 killed two other chaps who were standing near me and only knocked me over.'

Pte Parsons is buried in Abbeville Communal Cemetery.

Private
Albert Victor Rogers

Private Rogers of 26 School Terrace, Newtown, Reading, was born in Chertsey and was the adopted son of Mr & Mrs Rowley of 15 School Terrace, Newtown. Before his enlistment in February 1916 he worked at Huntley & Palmers. He joined the 8th Battalion of the Royal Berkshire Regiment in France in June 1916 and was initially reported missing on 18 August. A Sergeant Jackson writing to his wife said:

> 'He was all right in the morning, as I saw him myself, but a shell came and blew a part of the trench in, burying a

lot of us. That was the last I saw of him.'

Pte Rogers was later reported as having been killed in action on 18 August 1916, aged 26, and his name is recorded on the Thiepval Memorial to the Missing.

Second Lieutenant
Francis Saxon Snell

Second Lieutenant Snell was the only son of Mr A Saxon Snell FRIBA and Mrs Saxon Snell of Cranford, Cookham Dean, Berkshire. He was educated at Felstead School and graduated from King's College, Cambridge. At the outbreak of war he joined the Public Schools Special Training Corps and subsequently the Inns of Court Officer Training Corps at Berkhamsted. After a short course at Wellington College he was gazetted to the 6th Battalion of the Royal Berkshire Regiment and on 2 April 1916 was transferred to the 8th Battalion. He spent a month in the trenches then took over a platoon and was promoted to bombing officer. On 11 July 1916 he was killed at the age of 29 by a shrapnel-burst whilst reconnoitering the road from Lozenge Wood to Contalmaison. He is buried in Fricourt British Cemetery.

Private
W Yates DCM MM

Private Yates went to France to join the 8th Battalion of the Royal Berkshire Regiment on 12 October 1915. He is first mentioned in the battalion War Diary as having led a patrol to discover whether there was any movement of the enemy near the Double Crassier sap at Loos. He

discovered an enemy working party in the end of the sap and returning at once he led a bombing party of three men and bombed them out. The enemy dispersed, pursued by Pte Yates, on his own, until he had exhausted his supply of bombs. For his bravery on this occasion he was awarded a 'Green Ticket' by the General Officer Commanding 1st Division. On 27 September 1916 it was recorded in the diary that he had been awarded the Distinguished Conduct Medal and the Military Medal.

The MM was awarded for an action in July 1916, when Pte Yates was carrying messages under heavy fire and stopped to attend wounded comrades. The *London Gazette* citation for the award of the DCM dated 20 October 1916 reads:

> 'For conspicuous gallantry. When a small party was holding an advanced strong point he repeatedly carried messages, rations and ammunition under intense shell-fire. Finally he was badly wounded.'

(The report in the *Berkshire Chronicle* indicates that this action was within one or two days of when he won the MM, possibly 11 to 14 July).

Pte Yates must subsequently have been transferred to the 6th Battalion as, when that battalion was disbanded on 6 February 1918, he is shown as transferring to the 5th Battalion. His career thereafter is a mystery: according to the 1914/15 Star lists in the Public Record Office he deserted on 5 November 1918. However an article in the regimental journal in 1971 refers to his medals having been donated to the museum and put on display there, hardly the action of a deserter.

Appendix II   Visiting the Somme battlefield today

The locations of many of the Royal Berkshire battalions' actions can be traced today with relative ease and with a modest amount of walking. The intention of this section is to provide an introductory guide to some of the battlefield areas mentioned in the main text. We have arranged the material in battalion order of first participation in the Somme campaign.

Essential companions on the battlefield are the French IGN Blue Series maps (1:2,500) details of which are given below. Also invaluable is the excellent commentary, with sketch maps and illustrations, provided by Martin & Mary Middlebrook in *The Somme Battlefields*, Penguin 1994.

6th Battalion

1 July 1916 at Montauban

Map: IGN 2408 est (Bray-sur-Somme)

From Carnoy take the road leading north out of the village towards Montauban. After some 1,000m look out on the right for a small clump of trees on a rough patch of ground beside the road. This is the site of the Carnoy craters, a reminder of the mining activity which went on here in 1915 and early 1916. It is also the position of the British front line on 1 July 1916. The attack front of the 8th Norfolks straddled the road at this point and the 6th Royal Berkshires were on their left, advancing northwards in the direction of the Mametz-Montauban road. No features remain in the fields today now that the Casino Point crater has been filled in.

From here drive up to the D64 Mametz-Montauban road and turn left. The line of the German trench Montauban Alley ran parallel to this ridge road about 250m to the north. After 500m in the direction of Mametz a field track goes off to the right. Walking this will take you to where the 6th Battalion completed their successful advance on 1 July by establishing posts overlooking Caterpillar Wood and Caterpillar Valley.

Caterpillar Wood looking north-east

19 July 1916 at Longueval and Delville Wood

Map: IGN 2408 est (Bray-sur-Somme)

To follow the approach to Longueval and Delville Wood made by the 6th Battalion early in the morning of 19 July take the road from Montauban on the eastern outskirts of the village in the direction of Bazentin le Grand. After 250m a field track goes off to the right. This, shown on the IGN map as the Chemin de Montauban, was the 'sunken road into Longueval' referred to by Captain Rochfort. A familiar feature to the troops who took part in the major attack in this area made at dawn on 14 July, this track offers in good weather today fine views of the Longueval-Bazentin ridge and the adjacent woods. After about 2,500m the track emerges on a minor road south of Longueval. Turn right here and take the second road on the left leading into the main square of the village. From there the road on the right leads towards Delville Wood. When the south-western edge of the wood appears you will see across the fields a stone marker indicating the point at which South African troops entered the wood on 15 July. This was also we assume the point of entry for the 6th Battalion on 19 July. The location of the battalion's actions on that day can be traced at least approximately by finding the marker stone for 'Princes Street' which stands in the wood almost directly behind the South African National Memorial and the military museum. It was just to the south of this ride that a line was established on the afternoon of 19 July.

Sunken road to Longueval

26 September – 6 October 1916 at Thiepval and Schwaben Redoubt

Maps: IGN 2408 ouest (Albert) for Aveluy
        IGN 2407 ouest (Bapaume ouest) for Thiepval/ Schwaben

Crucifix Corner

During the 18th Division's attack on Thiepval the 6th Battalion was in reserve and their task was to provide carrying parties. Their dug-outs were located near Crucifix Corner, a point which can be visited by taking the minor road which leads west from the D929 Albert-Bapaume road at La Boisselle in the direction of Aveluy. At the junction with the D20 and the D151 the present-day crucifix can be seen in the trees on the right. From here tracks led up to the front-line positions at Thiepval.

The 6th Battalion moved into the front line on 28 September following the capture of the Schwaben Redoubt. The area occupied by this German strong point can be identified at least in its general aspect by following the D151 up to Thiepval and continuing north through the village for some 400m to where a small communal cemetery is situated in the triangle between the road and a track leading off to the left. This track leads up to the ridge overlooking Mill Road Cemetery and Thiepval Wood. On the reverse slope to the right were the fortifications of the Schwaben Redoubt. The 6th Battalion went into the line at a point which can be identified by going back to the D151 and driving (or walking!) 500m further up the road to a farm on the right. A track leads off to the right between the buildings to where a line of trees marks off the farm enclosure. The ground on the left of this track just beyond the trees is where 'B' Company of the Royal Berkshires occupied front line trenches until 6 October.

5th Battalion

3 July 1916 at Ovillers

Map: IGN 2408 ouest (Albert)

To locate the area of the 5th Battalion's unsuccessful attack on 3 July take the minor road from the D929 at La Boisselle leading west in the direction of Aveluy. For the first 700m you will be traversing Mash Valley with a view to the right towards the objectives on 1 July and again on 3 July: the village of Ovillers and its ridge. The minor road on the right which then leads to Ovillers is the 'sunken road' referred to by Lt-Col Willan in his letter to the Gold family. The 5th Battalion's front on 3 July

Sunken road
to Ovillers

straddled the road and a walk in the direction of Ovillers
Cemetery and the village shows clearly how the banks (more
prominent then than now) would have offered protection to
troops sheltering from German fire across open ground. Along
this road Lt-Col Willan and Lt Gold organised the withdrawal of
surviving members of the 5th Battalion and it was here that Lt
Gold was killed.

8 August 1916 at Pozières

Map: IGN 2407 est (Bapaume est)

The area in which the German attacks of 8 August against the
Royal Berkshire trenches were carried out is located between
the villages of Pozières and Courcelette. From the D929 Albert-
Bapaume road in Pozières take the D73 in the direction of
Thiepval. At the end of the village a track on the right forms a
Y-junction with the road. Follow this track which bends to the
right after some 200m. After 100m take the left fork and 750m
further along this track the fields on the right are the location of
the German attacks on Ration Trench and Fifth Avenue which
involved the use of Flammenwerfer. Mouquet Farm lies across
the fields to the left. To the right is the village of Courcelette.

8th Battalion

12–14 July 1916 at Contalmaison

Map: IGN 2408 est (Bray-sur-Somme)

The 8th Battalion's position from 12–14 July can readily be identified on the present D20 from Contalmaison to Mametz Wood. Where the main road bends sharply to the right just north of the village a minor road continues straight ahead past a water tower. This was the sunken road known as the Cutting which was occupied at 6.00 am on 12 July by a patrol of the 8th Battalion. The stretch of the D20 from this corner to the western edge of Mametz Wood, a distance of about 750m, corresponds to the line occupied by the battalion on the evening of 12 July and it was here that Lt-Col Dalby was wounded. From this road patrols were sent out northwards to Pearl Wood and Lower Wood, then in No Man's Land. Both woods can be seen today from the road, Lower Wood to the right, Pearl Wood nearer to Contalmaison. Pearl Alley, the former German communication trench along which the attack was made on 14 July, ran diagonally south-west to north-east across this ground and behind Pearl Wood.

3 September 1916 at High Wood

Map: IGN 2408 est (Bray-sur-Somme)

Memorial to the 1st Battalions of the Cameron Highlanders and the Black Watch at High Wood

The site of the 8th Battalion's action at High Wood on 3 September can also be visited from the D20, taking the road as far as the outskirts of Longueval where the D107 on the left leads up to the wood. As the road approaches the south-east corner of High Wood it runs parallel to the line of Rifles Trench close by in the fields on the right. The 8th Battalion moved into support here on 2 September. A track leads along the south-eastern edge of High Wood past a memorial to the Cameron Highlanders and the Black Watch. Joining the 1st Battalion of the Camerons on 3 September were two companies of the 8th Royal Berkshires and their joint objective was Wood Lane, a German trench running from High Wood south-east towards Longueval. Today a track leads off to the right just beyond the memorial; the line of Wood Lane ran in parallel about 50m to the north-east, converging with the track after 700m. The Camerons and the Royal Berkshires took Wood Lane on 3 September but had to retire to their original line following a German counter-attack.

Appendix III   Casualties and Commemorations

These tables were compiled from several official publications, together with records from the Commonwealth War Graves Commission and the Public Record Office. In some instances, there are variations between the sources in details such as service numbers, spelling of names and dates. In these cases, the most probable version has been used. A blank space indicates that the information was not available at the time of publication. The lists of men killed in action are set out in date order rather than alphabetically. We have chosen this presentation in order to show the impact on the battalions of the actions the men were engaged in during 1916.

The column headed 'Battalion location' indicates the whereabouts of the battalion on the date of the casualty, as stated in the appropriate War Diary. It will not necessarily be the place where a soldier was killed, as he or his company may have been on detachment remote from the battalion HQ at the time. The location has not been included in the tables of men who died of wounds.

During 1916, some 3,000 men in the three battalions were wounded and their names appeared in casualty lists in local newspapers. However, by July 1916, the battalion numbers were no longer published. While many of these names have been recorded by the authors, we do not feel that the information we have is sufficiently complete or accurate enough to warrant inclusion here. We would however be pleased to respond to researchers' enquiries.

5th Battalion

Killed in action

Date	Name	Rank	Number	Birthplace	Cemetery name	Battalion location
10/01/1916	Martin, Henry	Pte	8938	Bedwyn	Guards' Cemetery	Béthune
13/01/1916	Deering, George	Pte	10491	Plaxtol	Guards' Cemetery	Le Quesnoy
15/01/1916	Eldridge, Herbert Arthur	Pte	15646	Warnborough	Dud Corner Cem	Le Quesnoy
20/01/1916	Knapp, William	Pte	10715	Cowley	Guards' Cemetery	Fontes
17/02/1916	Davis, Arthur	Pte	10551	Whitepond	Loos Memorial	Noyelles
02/03/1916	Carter, William Edward	Pte	10353	Abingdon	Vermelles Brit Cem	Noyelles
02/03/1916	Irons, John William	L/Cpl	10612	Islington	Vermelles Brit Cem	Noyelles
02/03/1916	Stokes, Victor John	L/Cpl	9761	Shelford	Vermelles Brit Cem	Noyelles
03/03/1916	Buckland, Frank Chester	Pte	9644	Longcott	Vermelles Brit Cem	Vermelles
05/03/1916	Sheldon, Harold	L/Sgt	11069	Willesden	Loos Memorial	Vermelles
06/03/1916	Gibbs, Percy	Pte	11052	Paddington	Loos Memorial	Noyelles
16/03/1916	Ashfield, Alfred Charles	Cpl	16400	Devizes	Vermelles Brit Cem	Sailly la Bourse
20/03/1916	Field, William	Cpl	10801	Marylebone	Loos Memorial	Noyelles
21/03/1916	Payne, William James	Pte	11386	Highbury	Vermelles Brit Cem	Noyelles
22/03/1916	Lewendon, John	Sgt	11026	Newbury	Quarry Cem	Noyelles
25/03/1916	Rosier, Tom	Pte	15893	Beedon	Vermelles Brit Cem	Noyelles
28/03/1916	Williams, Edwin Albert	Pte	11060	Chelsea	Loos Memorial	Noyelles
31/03/1916	Bennett, John	Pte	10798	Wood Green	Loos Memorial	Noyelles
31/03/1916	Hale, Arthur	Cpl	10863	Skipton	Vermelles Brit Cem	Noyelles
31/03/1916	Nuccoll, William	Pte	16513	Cookham	Vermelles Brit Cem	Noyelles
31/03/1916	Pimm, George	L/Cpl	11241	Stanton Harcourt	Vermelles Brit Cem	Noyelles
31/03/1916	Walton, Thomas	A/Sgt	9205	Gornal	Vermelles Brit Cem	Noyelles
01/04/1916	Constable, Edward Victor	Pte	12204	Kentish Town	Vermelles Brit Cem	Noyelles
01/04/1916	Durndell, Percy	L/Cpl	11989	Brighton	Vermelles Brit Cem	Noyelles
01/04/1916	Simmons, Percy	Pte	9562	Peterborough	Vermelles Brit Cem	Noyelles
01/04/1916	West, Edward	Pte	10522	Wrotham	Vermelles Brit Cem	Noyelles
02/04/1916	Combley, Philip Walter	Pte	9792	Whitchurch	Vermelles Brit Cem	Noyelles
02/04/1916	Pullen, Oscar Albert	Pte	18722	Highgate	Vermelles Brit Cem	Noyelles
14/04/1916	Hawkins, Sydney	Pte	4585	Godshill IOW	Loos Memorial	Vermelles
16/04/1916	Johnson, Edward Frederick	Pte	16892	Windsor	Vermelles Brit Cem	Vermelles
18/04/1916	Ware, Francis Henry	Pte	10269	Reading	Vermelles Brit Cem	Vermelles
19/04/1916	Bolton, Richard	Pte	8040	Hull	Vermelles Brit Cem	Vermelles
20/04/1916	McManus, Peter Joseph	Pte	10766	Dundee	Vermelles Brit Cem	Vermelles
26/05/1916	Champ, Frederick Joseph	Pte	19011	Sunningwell	Philosophe Brit Cem	Vermelles
01/06/1916	Stonnill, Russell	Pte	11901	Yeovil	Noeux-les-Mines Comm Cem	Vermelles
02/06/1916	Appleton, Albert George	Pte	16845	Baughurst	St Patricks Cem Loos	Mazingarbe
02/06/1916	Dixey, William	Pte	11218	Bampton	St Patricks Cem Loos	Mazingarbe
02/06/1916	Walker, Henry John	Pte	16031	Reading	St Patricks Cem Loos	Mazingarbe
03/07/1916	Alderthay, Henry	Pte	16949	Smethwick	Thiepval Memorial	Attack on Ovillers
03/07/1916	Allden, Oliver	Pte	17558	Rotherhithe	Ovillers Mil Cem	Attack on Ovillers
03/07/1916	Barrett, James Edward	Pte	9460	Hackney	Thiepval Memorial	Attack on Ovillers
03/07/1916	Baverstock, Herbert Henry	Pte	11022	Hurstborne	Thiepval Memorial	Attack on Ovillers
03/07/1916	Bennett, Charles	L/Cpl	10865	Whitchurch	Thiepval Memorial	Attack on Ovillers
03/07/1916	Bramley, Charles Hugh	Pte	10520	Lound	Thiepval Memorial	Attack on Ovillers
03/07/1916	Brown, Brice	Pte	16618	Gt Shefford	Thiepval Memorial	Attack on Ovillers
03/07/1916	Butler, Aubrey Edward	2/Lieut			Thiepval Memorial	Attack on Ovillers
03/07/1916	Cable, William Walter	L/Sgt	11441	Lewisham	Thiepval Memorial	Attack on Ovillers
03/07/1916	Cannon, Edward Charles	Pte	19682	Wokingham	Thiepval Memorial	Attack on Ovillers
03/07/1916	Chapman, Charles William	L/Cpl	11044	Gt Bromley	Thiepval Memorial	Attack on Ovillers
03/07/1916	Chapman, Horace James	Pte	11691	Marlow	Thiepval Memorial	Attack on Ovillers
03/07/1916	Clarke, George Cecil	Pte	10632	Islington	Thiepval Memorial	Attack on Ovillers
03/07/1916	Coford, Thomas	Pte	11125	Stepney	Ovillers Mil Cem	Attack on Ovillers
03/07/1916	Cole, Sydney	Pte	10817	Forrest Hill Kent	Thiepval Memorial	Attack on Ovillers
03/07/1916	Cooper, Henry Charles	Pte	19615	Bradley	Thiepval Memorial	Attack on Ovillers
03/07/1916	Courtier, Frank Alfred	Pte	10688	Kennington	Thiepval Memorial	Attack on Ovillers
03/07/1916	Dury, Francis Stuart	L/Cpl	10731	St.Pancras	Thiepval Memorial	Attack on Ovillers
03/07/1916	Eastwood, Frederick Adolph	Pte	11544	Stockwell	Ovillers Mil Cem	Attack on Ovillers
03/07/1916	Edwards, Ebenezer	Pte	15681	Neath	Ovillers Mil Cem	Attack on Ovillers
03/07/1916	Enoch, Arthur	Pte	19433	Appleton	Thiepval Memorial	Attack on Ovillers
03/07/1916	Evans, Ernest	Pte	10425	Tilehurst	Ovillers Mil Cem	Attack on Ovillers
03/07/1916	Fern, Sydney George	Pte	10699	Forest Gate	Thiepval Memorial	Attack on Ovillers
03/07/1916	Filce, Alfred William	Pte	11545	Lambeth	Thiepval Memorial	Attack on Ovillers
03/07/1916	Flint, Alfred David	Pte	11047	Watford	Thiepval Memorial	Attack on Ovillers
03/07/1916	Giles, Edward Victor	2/Lieut			Thiepval Memorial	Attack on Ovillers
03/07/1916	Giles, George	Pte	10259	Garford	Thiepval Memorial	Attack on Ovillers
03/07/1916	Gold, Cecil Argo	Lieut			Aveluy Comm Cem Ext	Attack on Ovillers
03/07/1916	Gorton, Benjamin	L/Cpl	17262	Forrest Gate	Thiepval Memorial	Attack on Ovillers
03/07/1916	Green, George	L/Cpl	15654	Beenham	Ovillers Mil Cem	Attack on Ovillers
03/07/1916	Grove, Archibald	Pte	11029	Cox Green	Thiepval Memorial	Attack on Ovillers
03/07/1916	Haase, Edward George	2/Lieut			Thiepval Memorial	Attack on Ovillers
03/07/1916	Hall, Arthur Thomas	L/Cpl	10935	Merchiston Australia	Thiepval Memorial	Attack on Ovillers
03/07/1916	Harding, Harold Alfred	Pte	18373	Leckhampton	Thiepval Memorial	Attack on Ovillers
03/07/1916	Harman, Charles	Pte	10423	Brentford	Thiepval Memorial	Attack on Ovillers
03/07/1916	Hart, William Alfred	A/Cpl	11211	Southwark	Ovillers Mil Cem	Attack on Ovillers
03/07/1916	Hawes, William John	L/Cpl	10936	Dalston	Thiepval Memorial	Attack on Ovillers
03/07/1916	Hayes, Alexander Henry	Pte	8077	Lee	Thiepval Memorial	Attack on Ovillers
03/07/1916	Haywood, George	Pte	10743	Birmingham	Thiepval Memorial	Attack on Ovillers
03/07/1916	Hill, Henry	Pte	19608	Abingdon	Thiepval Memorial	Attack on Ovillers
03/07/1916	Hilsdon, William Thomas	L/Cpl	10285	Sutton Courtenay	Thiepval Memorial	Attack on Ovillers
03/07/1916	Kearse, Ernest	Pte	19679	Reading	Thiepval Memorial	Attack on Ovillers
03/07/1916	Keene, John	Pte	15258	Wallingford	Thiepval Memorial	Attack on Ovillers
03/07/1916	Kimbrey, Percival Eustace	Pte	19722	Reading	Thiepval Memorial	Attack on Ovillers
03/07/1916	King, George	Pte	16447	Cookham	Thiepval Memorial	Attack on Ovillers

Date	Name	Rank	Number	Birthplace	Cemetery name	Battalion location
03/07/1916	King, James William	Pte	18231	Poplar	Thiepval Memorial	Attack on Ovillers
03/07/1916	Knight, Harry Frederick	Pte	18401	Southampton	Thiepval Memorial	Attack on Ovillers
03/07/1916	Knight, Henry	Pte	10859	Reading	Thiepval Memorial	Attack on Ovillers
03/07/1916	Lloyd, Ernest William	L/Sgt	10734	Hurst	Thiepval Memorial	Attack on Ovillers
03/07/1916	Lloyd, Richard	Pte	10922	Bethnall Grn	Thiepval Memorial	Attack on Ovillers
03/07/1916	Lovett, Arthur Ernest	Pte	10682	Ilford	Thiepval Memorial	Attack on Ovillers
03/07/1916	Merry, Ernest	Pte	18301	Abingdon	Ovillers Mil Cem	Attack on Ovillers
03/07/1916	Messinger, Francis	Pte	15666	Goggsleas	Thiepval Memorial	Attack on Ovillers
03/07/1916	Moore, John Thomas	Pte	10940	Bethnal Grn	Thiepval Memorial	Attack on Ovillers
03/07/1916	Newton, Arthur	L/Cpl	15677		Thiepval Memorial	Attack on Ovillers
03/07/1916	Oglesby, William Henry	Pte	11088	Tottenham	Thiepval Memorial	Attack on Ovillers
03/07/1916	Owen, William Henry	Sgt	6514	Thatcham	Thiepval Memorial	Attack on Ovillers
03/07/1916	Palmer, Frank	Cpl	11327	Binfield	Thiepval Memorial	Attack on Ovillers
03/07/1916	Panting, Christopher John	Pte	19257	Inkpen	Thiepval Memorial	Attack on Ovillers
03/07/1916	Parker, Charles	Pte	11199	Walsall	Thiepval Memorial	Attack on Ovillers
03/07/1916	Partridge, Alec John	2/Lieut			Thiepval Memorial	Attack on Ovillers
03/07/1916	Patey, Stanley James	Pte	9657	Emmer Green	Thiepval Memorial	Attack on Ovillers
03/07/1916	Percy, Harry John	Pte	16952	North Kensington	Thiepval Memorial	Attack on Ovillers
03/07/1916	Plumb, George	Pte	11923	Mile End	Thiepval Memorial	Attack on Ovillers
03/07/1916	Popejoy, Arthur	Pte	16753	Aldermaston	Ovillers Mil Cem	Attack on Ovillers
03/07/1916	Radley, Bertie	Pte	11138	Bow	Thiepval Memorial	Attack on Ovillers
03/07/1916	Rance, George Thomas	Pte	19661	Bracknell	Thiepval Memorial	Attack on Ovillers
03/07/1916	Rivers, Robert	Pte	19106	Longworth	Thiepval Memorial	Attack on Ovillers
03/07/1916	Rose, Amos	L/Cpl	10748	Wandsworth	Ovillers Mil Cem	Attack on Ovillers
03/07/1916	Rosier, Harold	Pte	15694	Hungerford	Thiepval Memorial	Attack on Ovillers
03/07/1916	Sargeant, Frederick	Pte	19420	Binfield	Thiepval Memorial	Attack on Ovillers
03/07/1916	Saunders, Vincent Elijah	Cpl	16063	Cholsey	Thiepval Memorial	Attack on Ovillers
03/07/1916	Scott, George	Pte	10826	Buckhurst Hill	Thiepval Memorial	Attack on Ovillers
03/07/1916	Seymour, Frank	Pte	10653		Thiepval Memorial	Attack on Ovillers
03/07/1916	Shenow, William	L/Cpl	17259	Whitechapel	Thiepval Memorial	Attack on Ovillers
03/07/1916	Shepherd, John George	Pte	11009	Oxford	Aveluy Comm Cem Ext	Attack on Ovillers
03/07/1916	Slade, James Edward	Pte	19004	Fawley	Thiepval Memorial	Attack on Ovillers
03/07/1916	Slaughter, Albert George	Pte	18720	Horsham	Thiepval Memorial	Attack on Ovillers
03/07/1916	Smith, Alfred Jesse	Pte	10549	Halling	Thiepval Memorial	Attack on Ovillers
03/07/1916	Smith, Arthur	Pte	6465	Reading	Thiepval Memorial	Attack on Ovillers
03/07/1916	Smith, Richard	Pte	11010	Wokingham	Thiepval Memorial	Attack on Ovillers
03/07/1916	Stewart, Humphrey	Capt			Thiepval Memorial	Attack on Ovillers
03/07/1916	Sumner, George William	Pte	7796	Windlesham	Thiepval Memorial	Attack on Ovillers
03/07/1916	Tanner, William	Pte	10862	Woodcote	Thiepval Memorial	Attack on Ovillers
03/07/1916	Tidbury, William	Pte	19583	Ramsbury	Thiepval Memorial	Attack on Ovillers
03/07/1916	Trott, George Eniss	Pte	11055	Barnett	Thiepval Memorial	Attack on Ovillers
03/07/1916	Tubb, Arthur	Pte	19590	Woodley	Thiepval Memorial	Attack on Ovillers
03/07/1916	Wackerill, Edward West	Pte	19034	Wandsworth	Thiepval Memorial	Attack on Ovillers
03/07/1916	Webb, Ernest Arthur	Pte	10515	Reading	Thiepval Memorial	Attack on Ovillers
03/07/1916	Webb, Robert Edward	Pte	10284	Paddington	Ovillers Mil Cem	Attack on Ovillers
03/07/1916	Wells, Joseph Charles	Pte	7941	Grays	Thiepval Memorial	Attack on Ovillers
03/07/1916	Whitehorn, Charles	Pte	17476	Newbury	Thiepval Memorial	Attack on Ovillers
03/07/1916	Wills, Arthur	Pte	12299	York	Thiepval Memorial	Attack on Ovillers
03/07/1916	Wilmer, Arthur Richard	Pte	10895	Stoke Newington	Thiepval Memorial	Attack on Ovillers
03/07/1916	Woodley, Charles	L/Cpl	5752	Reading	Thiepval Memorial	Attack on Ovillers
08/07/1916	Collins, William George	Pte	10449	Aston	Thiepval Memorial	Bouzincourt
19/07/1916	Butler, Elijah Thomas	L/Cpl	19133	East Hagbourne	Thiepval Memorial	Bois du Warnicourt
19/07/1916	Oakes, Albert Edwin	Pte	24062	Brownhills	Thiepval Memorial	Bois du Warnicourt
19/07/1916	Saunders, Charles Herbert	Pte	10673	Shoreditch	Caterpillar Valley Cem	Bois du Warnicourt
30/07/1916	Barnett, Charles	Pte	19961	Great Tew	Thiepval Memorial	Bouzincourt
30/07/1916	Coleman, William Charles	Pte	10464	Nettlebed	Guillemont Rd Cem	Bouzincourt
30/07/1916	Dance, William	Pte	21000	Hurst	Tincourt New Brit Cem	Bouzincourt
30/07/1916	Herbert, Harvey George	Pte	21317	Curridge	Thiepval Memorial	Bouzincourt
30/07/1916	Miles, George Edwin	Pte	20957	Hurst	Thiepval Memorial	Bouzincourt
30/07/1916	Taylor, William	Pte	19269	Litchfield	Thiepval Memorial	Bouzincourt
06/08/1916	Brant, William	L/Sgt	11341	Wokingham	Thiepval Memorial	Trenches at Pozières
08/08/1916	Barnes, Walter Francis	Pte	17737	Reading	Thiepval Memorial	Trenches at Pozières
08/08/1916	Briggs, George Harold	Pte	17223	Sevend	Thiepval Memorial	Trenches at Pozières
08/08/1916	Brooks, William	Pte	10304	Kingston Bagpuize	Thiepval Memorial	Trenches at Pozières
08/08/1916	Clarke, Charles	Pte	15644	Beenham	Thiepval Memorial	Trenches at Pozières
08/08/1916	Davis, Arthur John	Pte	10786	Horfield	Thiepval Memorial	Trenches at Pozières
08/08/1916	Dray, Herbert Arthur	L/Cpl	23564	St Leonards on Sea	Thiepval Memorial	Trenches at Pozières
08/08/1916	Goodwin, Albert Louis	Pte	19641	Birchington	Thiepval Memorial	Trenches at Pozières
08/08/1916	Hemmett, Frederick Charles	Pte	23669	Birmingham	Thiepval Memorial	Trenches at Pozières
08/08/1916	Hughes, Gordon McGregor	2/Lieut			Thiepval Memorial	Trenches at Pozières
08/08/1916	Lawrence, Frank	Pte	10265	Newbury	Thiepval Memorial	Trenches at Pozières
08/08/1916	Paddock, Gerfield	Pte	23666	Edmonton	Thiepval Memorial	Trenches at Pozières
08/08/1916	Peckover, Harold William	Pte	19622	Burough	Serre Road No 2 Cem	Trenches at Pozières
08/08/1916	Pritchard, John Stanley	Pte	23578	Wooton under Edge	Regina Trench Cem	Trenches at Pozières
08/08/1916	Scott, Harold Edmund	Pte	23608	Portsmouth	Thiepval Memorial	Trenches at Pozières
08/08/1916	Thorpe, Alfred Victor	Pte	20121	Newport	Thiepval Memorial	Trenches at Pozières
08/08/1916	Toogood, Arthur	Pte	23599	Newport IOW	Thiepval Memorial	Trenches at Pozières
08/08/1916	Uttley, Walter John	Pte	23700	Portsmouth	Pozières Brit Cem	Trenches at Pozières
08/08/1916	Wake, Herbert Charles	Pte	15639	Abingdon	Pozières Brit Cem	Trenches at Pozières
08/08/1916	Walter, James Bertram	Pte	16866	Croydon	Pozières Brit Cem	Trenches at Pozières
08/08/1916	Wicks, James William	Pte	49454	Hurst	Thiepval Memorial	Trenches at Pozières
09/08/1916	Bance, Robert Arman	2/Lieut			Bapaume Post Mil Cem	Trenches at Pozières
09/08/1916	Burt, Jack	Pte	11358	Blandford	Bouzincourt Comm Cem Ext	Trenches at Pozières
09/08/1916	Griffin, John	L/Cpl	10717	Hungerford	Pozières Brit Cem	Trenches at Pozières
09/08/1916	Hart, Reginald Percy	Pte	23659	Swindon	Thiepval Memorial	Trenches at Pozières
09/08/1916	Jones, Mathew Alfred	Pte	23715	Shrewsbury	Pozières Brit Cem	Trenches at Pozières
09/08/1916	Lefevre, Joseph William	L/Cpl	10845	Hoxton	Thiepval Memorial	Trenches at Pozières

Date	Name	Rank	Number	Birthplace	Cemetery name	Battalion location
09/08/1916	Lovell, John William	Pte	23667	Fareham	Thiepval Memorial	Trenches at Pozières
09/08/1916	Moore, Stanley	Pte	24201	Warminster	Thiepval Memorial	Trenches at Pozières
09/08/1916	Oakes, Leonard	Pte	23635	Swindon	Thiepval Memorial	Trenches at Pozières
18/08/1916	McCumskay, John	Pte	14065	London	Pozières Brit Cem	Wanquentin
18/08/1916	Morris, William	Pte	14982	West Bromwich	Thiepval Memorial	Wanquentin
25/08/1916	Wingrove, Ralph	L/Cpl	10481	Penn	Arras Memorial	Trenches in front of Arras
26/08/1916	Denbow, Harry Robert	Pte	10793	Blackfriars	Péronne Road Cem	Trenches in front of Arras
26/08/1916	Kimbrey, Percival Eustace	Pte	19722	Reading	Thiepval Memorial	Trenches in front of Arras
28/08/1916	Archard, Arthur Henry	Pte	22323	Bradford-on-Avon	Thiepval Memorial	Trenches in front of Arras
26/09/1916	Wilbraham, Taylor Aucher	2/Lieut			Arras Memorial	Trenches in front of Arras
09/10/1916	Evans, John Walter	Pte	15664	Birmingham	Thiepval Memorial	Flers trench nr Longueval
09/10/1916	Ferguson, Gilbert	Pte	15216	Islington	Guards Cemetery	Flers trench nr Longueval
10/10/1916	Knight, Stanley Edwin	Pte	8699	Windsor	Bancourt British Cem	Flers trench nr Longueval
12/10/1916	Fossey, Albert	Pte	10946	Paddington	Thiepval Memorial	Flers trench nr Longueval
13/10/1916	Cobb, Reginald	2/Lieut			Bulls Road Cemetery	Flers trench nr Longueval
14/10/1916	Perkins, Thomas Alfred	CSM	6589	Gosport	Bulls Road Cemetery	Flers trench nr Longueval
14/10/1916	Taylor, Harry	Pte	23579	Salisbury	Bulls Road Cemetery	Flers trench nr Longueval
14/10/1916	Tryhorn, William	Pte	18967	Ashford	Bulls Road Cemetery	Flers trench nr Longueval
14/10/1916	Tucker, William Thomas	Pte	18487	Newbury	Bulls Road Cemetery	Flers trench nr Longueval
14/10/1916	Walker, George Henry	Pte	23694	Birmingham	Guards Cemetery	Flers trench nr Longueval
15/10/1916	Belcher, William Henry	Pte	19447	Great Coxwell	Thiepval Memorial	Flers trench nr Longueval
15/10/1916	Eyles, Thomas Charles	Pte	22322	Lambourne	Thiepval Memorial	Flers trench nr Longueval
15/10/1916	Rowland, Thomas	Pte	20178	Sparsholt	Beaulencourt British Cem	Flers trench nr Longueval
18/10/1916	Bailey, James	Sgt	17946	Uffington	Guards Cemetery	Flers trench nr Longueval
18/10/1916	Ellis, William Richard	Pte	19118	Aston	Thiepval Memorial	Flers trench nr Longueval
18/10/1916	McGuire, Percy	Pte	13671	Stepney	Thiepval Memorial	Flers trench nr Longueval
19/10/1916	Bumstead, George	Pte	17280	Needham Market	Thiepval Memorial	Mametz Wood
19/10/1916	Critton, John	Pte	19611	Clerkenwell	Thiepval Memorial	Mametz Wood
19/10/1916	Farr, George	Pte	10967	Bethnal Grn	Thiepval Memorial	Mametz Wood
19/10/1916	Fricker, William John	Pte	23678	East Knoyle	Thiepval Memorial	Mametz Wood
19/10/1916	Hopkins, Wilfred James	Pte	23632	Southampton	Thiepval Memorial	Mametz Wood
19/10/1916	Mendham, Lewis	Pte	23634	Portsmouth	Thiepval Memorial	Mametz Wood
19/10/1916	Porter, Leonard William	Pte	17670	Edmonton	Thiepval Memorial	Mametz Wood
19/10/1916	Willcox, Harold	L/Cpl	10536	Gillingham	Thiepval Memorial	Mametz Wood
22/10/1916	White, Frederick	Pte	18477	Sunningdale	Thiepval Memorial	Hauteville
24/11/1916	Edwards, Arthur	Pte	12857	Barton	Faubourg d'Amiens Cem	In trenches near Arras
02/12/1916	Allen, James	Pte	27139	Stratfield Saye	Faubourg d'Amiens Cem	In trenches near Arras
02/12/1916	Barlow, Henry	Pte	25532	Reading	Faubourg d'Amiens Cem	In trenches near Arras
02/12/1916	Honeybone, Victor Harry	Pte	39347	Ascott under Wychwood	Faubourg d'Amiens Cem	In trenches near Arras
02/12/1916	Warren, William	Pte	18249	Rotherhithe	Faubourg d'Amiens Cem	In trenches near Arras
05/12/1916	Brogden, Charles	Pte	25523	Cumnor	Faubourg d'Amiens Cem	Billets in Arras
05/12/1916	Chivers, Harry	Sgt	10256	Colnbrook	Faubourg d'Amiens Cem	Billets in Arras
05/12/1916	Timms, William James	L/Sgt	8445	Kidlington	Faubourg d'Amiens Cem	Billets in Arras
11/12/1916	Trodd, Laurence Richard	Pte	37375	Odiham	Wanquetin Comm Cem Ext	In trenches near Arras

Died of wounds

Date	Name	Rank	Number	Birthplace	Cemetery name
20/04/1916	Appleford, Alfred Henry	Pte	16409	Baydon	Vermelles Brit Cem
03/03/1916	Bagland, Sydney	Pte	11068	Birmingham	Vermelles Brit Cem
16/04/1916	Ball, William	Pte	17268	Bermondsey	Béthune Town Cem
25/10/1916	Betteridge, Frederick Alfred	Pte	18737	Clewer	Etaples Mil Cem
07/03/1916	Bew, Brice	Pte	15928	Newbury	Newbury Municipal Cem
20/04/1916	Birkby, Henry Alexander	2/Lieut			Béthune Town Cem
16/08/1916	Boyce, Innes Douglas	A/Sgt	11914	Shalford	Puchevillers Brit Cem
09/07/1916	Brown, Harold Masters	2/Lieut			Etaples Mil Cem
18/03/1916	Capon, Edward	L/Cpl	10749	Tooting	Calais Southern Cem
14/01/1916	Clark, Frederick	Sgt	11145	Plaistow	Béthune Town Cem
18/10/1916	Cowley, Charles	Pte	23657	Wroughton	Longueval Road Cem
10/08/1916	Edwards, Francis Andrew Lloyd	2/Lieut			Puchevillers Brit Cem
26/07/1916	Fage, George	Pte	10592	Bloomsbury	All Saints Wokingham
20/10/1916	Faithfull, George Stevens	Pte	17226	Winkfield	Heilly Station Cemetery
04/10/1916	Forrest, James Herbert John	Pte	13105	Swindon	Longueval Road Cem
14/10/1916	Gibbs, James Frederick	Pte	19783	Hungerford	Bulls Road Cemetery
19/11/1916	Hainge, Arthur George	Pte	23714	Birmingham	Barly French Mil Cem
02/12/1916	Harvey, George	Pte	18067	Leamington	Faubourg d'Amiens Cem
17/01/1916	Hawtin, Henry	Pte	7783	Benson	Béthune Town Cem
28/07/1916	Howse, Walter	Pte	15296	Cholsey	St Marys Cholsey
28/11/1916	Hutchings, William	Cpl	16032	Reading	Wanquetin Comm Cem
13/07/1916	James, Joe Conquest	Capt			Wimereux Comm Cem
24/10/1916	Keep, Percy	Pte	19671	Burghfield	Heilly Station Cemetery
19/07/1916	Kenody, William Reuben	Pte	11808	Reading	Etaples Mil Cem
26/02/1916	Knight, James William	Pte	18502	Burnham	Béthune Town Cem
18/12/1916	Lambert, William	Pte	25536	Clewer	Wanquetin Comm Cem Ext
22/03/1916	MacGregor, Herbert Austin	Pte	19287	Wyck Ressington	Etaples Mil Cem
03/04/1916	Maslin, Thomas	Pte	15862	Reading	Vermelles Brit Cem
05/05/1916	Maslin, Thomas	Pte	15862	Reading	Vermelles Brit Cem
20/08/1916	Mould, William	Pte	23679	Salisbury	St Sever Cem
19/10/1916	Pawling, Reynard	Pte	19407	Littleworth	Heilly Station Cemetery
28/08/1916	Phipps, Frederick	Pte	11064	Wood Grn	St Sever Cem
15/10/1916	Pigott, Edward Francis	Pte	11186	Brooksland NY	Douai Comm Cem
11/08/1916	Powell, Robert	Sgt	10428	Lockinge	Etaples Mil Cem
21/04/1916	Purcell, Ernest Edwin	Pte	16878	Hampstead	Béthune Town Cem
09/08/1916	Robinson, Edward Arthur	Pte	20144	Watlington	Warloy Baillon Comm Cem Ext

Date	Name	Rank	Number	Birthplace	Cemetery name
16/10/1916	Rolls, William	Pte	19620	Wantage	Longueval Road Cem
29/03/1916	Seymour, Christopher William	Pte	10197	Beenham	Calais Southern Cem
01/11/1916	Sims, Edward James	Cpl	14378	Wantage	St Sever Cem Ext
25/05/1916	Splarn, Walter William	Pte	10624	Marylebone	Lapugnoy Mil Cem
02/07/1916	Stannett, Bernard William	Pte	19176	Windsor	Touchen End Cemetery
26/04/1916	Swain, Alfred Benjamin	Pte	11194	East Ham	St Mary Magdalene East Ham
25/04/1916	Swift, William	Pte	19505	Stepney	St Sever Cem
06/11/1916	Teale, Allan Rowland	Pte	10044	Brentford	Etaples Mil Cem
22/03/1916	Thomas, John	Pte	9778	Oxford	Béthune Town Cem
31/05/1916	Thorns, Francis Joseph	2/Lieut			Noeux-les-Mines Comm Cem
03/07/1916	Wace, Percival Beckwith	Capt			Thiepval Memorial
21/05/1916	White, Ernest	Clr Sgt	20655	Birmingham	Parkhurst Mil Cem (Newport)
13/07/1916	Wilde, John	Pte	18168	Stockport	Lawns Wood Cemetery Leeds
04/01/1916	Woodbridge, Edgar Harry	A/CSM	8229	Faringdon	Calais Southern Cem

6th Battalion

Killed in action

Date	Name	Rank	Number	Birthplace	Cemetery name	Battalion location
10/01/1916	Kerrins, Thomas Joseph	Pte	12551	Sligo	Bécourt Military Cem	La Boisselle
10/01/1916	Sanders, Alfred	Pte	15349	Maidenhead	Bécourt Military Cem	La Boisselle
24/01/1916	Freston, Hugh Reginald	2/Lieut			Bécourt Military Cem	La Boisselle
08/02/1916	Brown, Oliver	Pte	12613	MantyCook USA	Bécourt Military Cem	La Boisselle
08/02/1916	Shawyer, William	Pte	13003	Putney	Bécourt Military Cem	La Boisselle
14/02/1916	Povey, William Robert	Pte	15403	Newbury	Bécourt Military Cem	Albert
28/02/1916	O'Brien, Michael	Pte	17501	Wellington NZ	Bécourt Military Cem	La Boisselle
10/03/1916	Garner, William	Pte	36566	Waterbeach	Adanac Military Cem	Frenchencourt
10/03/1916	Hankin, Philip	Pte	36576	Cambridge	Adanac Military Cemetery	Frenchencourt
27/03/1916	Morton, William	Pte	17473	Marylebone	Cerisy-Gailly Mil Cem	Maricourt Defences
27/03/1916	Root, Christian Harry	Pte	12144	Bethnal Green	Cerisy-Gailly Mil Cem	Maricourt Defences
30/03/1916	Bird, Walter	Pte	12260	Birmingham	Cerisy-Gailly Mil Cem	Maricourt Defences
07/04/1916	McGlade, Wilfred	Pte	12089	Caterham	Cerisy-Gailly Mil Cem	Maricourt Defences
19/04/1916	Bonser, Sidney Benjamin	Pte	15407	Woolwich	Cerisy-Gailly Mil Cem	Z2 Sector Maricourt
19/04/1916	Bullin, William Arthur	Pte	19468	Westminster	Cerisy-Gailly Mil Cem	Z2 Sector Maricourt
19/04/1916	Chittock, Albert Ralph	Pte	12141	Canning Town	Cerisy-Gailly Mil Cem	Z2 Sector Maricourt
19/04/1916	Cordeaux, Albert	Pte	11164	Bermondsey	Cerisy-Gailly Mil Cem	Z2 Sector Maricourt
19/04/1916	James, Arthur Thomas	Pte	12549	Westminster	Cerisy-Gailly Mil Cem	Z2 Sector Maricourt
26/05/1916	Compton, Charles Ernest	Pte	12510	Lambeth	Carnoy Military Cem	Sector A2 Carnoy
03/06/1916	Winter, Harry	L/Cpl	11488	Colney	Carnoy Military Cem	Billetts in Bray
21/06/1916	Hadley, Joseph	Pte	12274	West Bromwich	Carnoy Military Cem	Sector A2 Carnoy
22/06/1916	Wayman, Henry	Pte	19547	E Dulwich	Carnoy Military Cem	Sector A2 Carnoy
29/06/1916	Atkins, William John	Pte	12646	Gowerton	Carnoy Military Cem	Sector A2 Carnoy
29/06/1916	Bailey, Henry John	Pte	12529	Holloway	Thiepval Memorial	Sector A2 Carnoy
29/06/1916	Davenport, Zacharia Bartley	Pte	13022	Northleach	Carnoy Military Cem	Sector A2 Carnoy
29/06/1916	Halley, Arthur	Pte	12395	Edgebaston	Carnoy Military Cem	Sector A2 Carnoy
29/06/1916	Spurring, Alfred Charles	Pte	12340	Birmingham	Thiepval Memorial	Sector A2 Carnoy
01/07/1916	Ash, Frederick George	Pte	12833	Clewer	Thiepval Memorial	Attack at Montauban
01/07/1916	Baker, Montague	Pte	25239	Folkestone	Thiepval Memorial	Attack at Montauban
01/07/1916	Barnsley, William	L/Cpl	12297	Oldbury	Thiepval Memorial	Attack at Montauban
01/07/1916	Bartlett, Alfred	Pte	10075	Wallingford	Thiepval Memorial	Attack at Montauban
01/07/1916	Bayley, Erskine Cochrane	2/Lieut			Carnoy Military Cem	Attack at Montauban
01/07/1916	Beckett, John	Pte	16711	Beedon	Thiepval Memorial	Attack at Montauban
01/07/1916	Biddle, Herbert Frederick	L/Sgt	12052	Islington	Thiepval Memorial	Attack at Montauban
01/07/1916	Broadhurst, Albert George	Pte	12898	Reading	Thiepval Memorial	Attack at Montauban
01/07/1916	Bryan, Phillip Alfred	Pte	12129	Hackney	Thiepval Memorial	Attack at Montauban
01/07/1916	Butcher, George Henry	Pte	12666	Rudry Glam	Thiepval Memorial	Attack at Montauban
01/07/1916	Bye, Frederick William	L/Sgt	12586	Islington	Thiepval Memorial	Attack at Montauban
01/07/1916	Carter, Ernest	Pte	14837	Maidenhead	Thiepval Memorial	Attack at Montauban
01/07/1916	Casey, Robert Charles	Pte	10139	St Pancras	Thiepval Memorial	Attack at Montauban
01/07/1916	Cawley, Frank	Pte	12227	Rotherhithe	Thiepval Memorial	Attack at Montauban
01/07/1916	Clarence, John	Pte	12270	Birmingham	Thiepval Memorial	Attack at Montauban
01/07/1916	Cole, Ernest George	L/Cpl	16402	Theale	Thiepval Memorial	Attack at Montauban
01/07/1916	Collot, Thomas Alexander	2/Lieut			Carnoy Military Cem	Attack at Montauban
01/07/1916	Collyer, William James	Pte	16587	Wokingham	Thiepval Memorial	Attack at Montauban
01/07/1916	Comley, Reginald Joseph	L/Sgt	12758	Oare	Dantzig Alley Brit Cem	Attack at Montauban
01/07/1916	Courage, Godfrey Mitchell	2/Lieut			Carnoy Military Cem	Attack at Montauban
01/07/1916	Cox, Frederick	Pte	16713	Spital	Thiepval Memorial	Attack at Montauban
01/07/1916	Craxton, Francis Frank	Pte	15350	Checkendon	Thiepval Memorial	Attack at Montauban
01/07/1916	Curtis, Thomas	Pte	16051	Kingston Lyle	Thiepval Memorial	Attack at Montauban
01/07/1916	Davis, John	Pte	16064	Reading	Thiepval Memorial	Attack at Montauban
01/07/1916	Dickinson, Robert Henry	Pte	12127	Woodford	Thiepval Memorial	Attack at Montauban
01/07/1916	Digby, Ernest Sidney	Pte	17503	Poplar	Thiepval Memorial	Attack at Montauban
01/07/1916	Dray, Frederick Charles	Pte	11331	East Grinstead	Thiepval Memorial	Attack at Montauban
01/07/1916	Eagleton, John Thomas	Pte	17500	Bethnal Grn	Thiepval Memorial	Attack at Montauban
01/07/1916	Edwards, Edward	Pte	12359	East Ham	Thiepval Memorial	Attack at Montauban
01/07/1916	Edwards, Walter Charles	Pte	13015	Ascot	Thiepval Memorial	Attack at Montauban
01/07/1916	Enoch, Thomas Humphrey	Pte	13018	Sutton Courtenay	Thiepval Memorial	Attack at Montauban
01/07/1916	Faulkner, Albert Victor	Pte	12501	Aston	Thiepval Memorial	Attack at Montauban
01/07/1916	Foulds, Edward James	Pte	12113	Hackney	Thiepval Memorial	Attack at Montauban
01/07/1916	Garner, George	Pte	12100	Bethnal Grn	Thiepval Memorial	Attack at Montauban
01/07/1916	Gilbert, William	Sgt	12310	West Bromwich	Thiepval Memorial	Attack at Montauban
01/07/1916	Glibbery, William	L/Cpl	12158	Poplar	Dantzig Alley Brit Cem	Attack at Montauban
01/07/1916	Glover, Alfred	Pte	12174	Clapton	Thiepval Memorial	Attack at Montauban
01/07/1916	Gray, Walter Frank	Pte	12116	Lewis	Dantzig Alley Brit Cem	Attack at Montauban

Date	Name	Rank	Number	Birthplace	Cemetery name	Battalion location
01/07/1916	Green, Richard	L/Cpl	12028	St. Pancras	Dantzig Alley Brit Cem	Attack at Montauban
01/07/1916	Harris, Joseph	Pte	14548	Eynsham	Thiepval Memorial	Attack at Montauban
01/07/1916	Harris, Maurice John	L/Sgt	12462	Hammersmith	Thiepval Memorial	Attack at Montauban
01/07/1916	Harrison, Thomas	L/Cpl	18543	Colne	Thiepval Memorial	Attack at Montauban
01/07/1916	Hayes, Harry Charles	L/Cpl	12071	Bermondsey	Thiepval Memorial	Attack at Montauban
01/07/1916	Hodges, George	Pte	15373	Fawley Bottom	Thiepval Memorial	Attack at Montauban
01/07/1916	Horsey, Alfred Frederick Fuller	L/Cpl	12463	Auckland NZ	Thiepval Memorial	Attack at Montauban
01/07/1916	Howe, Charles Kingsley	2/Lieut			Carnoy Military Cem	Attack at Montauban
01/07/1916	Hurn, Frederick Everett	Sgt	10365	Wooburn	Thiepval Memorial	Attack at Montauban
01/07/1916	Jones, Stanley Norman	Cpl	12642	Dawley	Thiepval Memorial	Attack at Montauban
01/07/1916	Jones, William	Pte	12390	Birmingham	La Neuville Brit Cem	Attack at Montauban
01/07/1916	Jones, William Hay	Pte	10205	Southwark	Thiepval Memorial	Attack at Montauban
01/07/1916	Knapp, Cecil Egbert	Cpl	12678	Newington	Thiepval Memorial	Attack at Montauban
01/07/1916	Lawrence, William Albert	Pte	16534	Headley	Thiepval Memorial	Attack at Montauban
01/07/1916	Litten, Raymond	Capt			Carnoy Military Cem	Attack at Montauban
01/07/1916	Lloyd, Edward	Pte	12345	Birmingham	Thiepval Memorial	Attack at Montauban
01/07/1916	Long, Frederick James	Pte	15391	Guildford	Thiepval Memorial	Attack at Montauban
01/07/1916	Long, George Thomas	Cpl	1209	Olslington	Dantzig Alley Brit Cem	Attack at Montauban
01/07/1916	Martin, Thomas	Pte	15387	Slough	Thiepval Memorial	Attack at Montauban
01/07/1916	Maynard, Arthur George	A/Sgt	13770	Lambeth	Thiepval Memorial	Attack at Montauban
01/07/1916	Maynard, George Richard	L/Cpl	12087	Wood Grn	Thiepval Memorial	Attack at Montauban
01/07/1916	Maysey, Frank	Pte	12427	Birmingham	Thiepval Memorial	Attack at Montauban
01/07/1916	McCullough, Albert James	Pte	12820	Reading	Thiepval Memorial	Attack at Montauban
01/07/1916	Merrix, George Arthur	Pte	12428	Birmingham	Dantzig Alley Brit Cem	Attack at Montauban
01/07/1916	Morgan, Hubert	Pte	11314	Stratford	Dantzig Alley Brit Cem	Attack at Montauban
01/07/1916	Nash, Leonard	Pte	12868	Wolverhampton	Thiepval Memorial	Attack at Montauban
01/07/1916	Nolan, William	Pte	12691	Liverpool	Thiepval Memorial	Attack at Montauban
01/07/1916	Nunn, Frederick	Pte	12049	Clerkenwell	Carnoy Military Cem	Attack at Montauban
01/07/1916	Orsgood, William Thomas	Pte	16714	Windsor	Thiepval Memorial	Attack at Montauban
01/07/1916	Provins, Jack	Pte	12856	Sandhurst	Thiepval Memorial	Attack at Montauban
01/07/1916	Pullinger, William	L/Cpl	12828	Winchester	Thiepval Memorial	Attack at Montauban
01/07/1916	Russell, Henry George	Pte	12862	Binfield	Thiepval Memorial	Attack at Montauban
01/07/1916	Sear, George	Pte	12075	Islington	Thiepval Memorial	Attack at Montauban
01/07/1916	Simmonds, John	Pte	10427	Reading	Thiepval Memorial	Attack at Montauban
01/07/1916	Skilton, George	Pte	12499	Westminster	Thiepval Memorial	Attack at Montauban
01/07/1916	Skudder, Joseph William	Pte	12996	Battersea	Thiepval Memorial	Attack at Montauban
01/07/1916	Smith, Frederick William	Pte	19610	Islington	Thiepval Memorial	Attack at Montauban
01/07/1916	Smith, George	Pte	16675	Ogbourne	Thiepval Memorial	Attack at Montauban
01/07/1916	Smith, Percy	L/Cpl	12488	Wellington	Thiepval Memorial	Attack at Montauban
01/07/1916	Souper, Noel Beaumont	2/Lieut			Thiepval Memorial	Attack at Montauban
01/07/1916	Speller, Henry William	A/CSM	12583	London	Thiepval Memorial	Attack at Montauban
01/07/1916	Stimpson, Walter	Pte	16197	Appleton	Thiepval Memorial	Attack at Montauban
01/07/1916	Syms, Albert Edward	L/Cpl	12519	Camberwell	Thiepval Memorial	Attack at Montauban
01/07/1916	Taylor, Frank	Pte	19678	Oare	Thiepval Memorial	Attack at Montauban
01/07/1916	Thoules, Richard William	Pte	12814	West Ham	Thiepval Memorial	Attack at Montauban
01/07/1916	Traill, Kenneth Robert	Lieut			Carnoy Military Cem	Attack at Montauban
01/07/1916	Watton, Thomas	Pte	12243	West Bromwich	Thiepval Memorial	Attack at Montauban
01/07/1916	Williams, Francis	Pte	12840	Hungerford	Thiepval Memorial	Attack at Montauban
01/07/1916	Wiseman, Frederick	Pte	12983	Long Melford	Thiepval Memorial	Attack at Montauban
10/07/1916	Stone, Charles Francis	Pte	12537	Southwark	St Sever Cem	Grovetown
18/07/1916	Easton, Charles Thomas	Pte	12718	London	Talus Boisé Longueval	
19/07/1916	Andrews, Edwin Joseph	Pte	13593	Hyde	Thiepval Memorial	Attack on Longueval
19/07/1916	Barton, Harry	L/Cpl	12304	Birmingham	Thiepval Memorial	Attack on Longueval
19/07/1916	Bourne, John Percy	Pte	12562	Droitwich	Thiepval Memorial	Attack on Longueval
19/07/1916	Brill, Walter Ernest	Pte	12854	Reading	Thiepval Memorial	Attack on Longueval
19/07/1916	Burgess, William Vernon	2/Lieut			Thiepval Memorial	Attack on Longueval
19/07/1916	Cordell, William James	L/Sgt	12931	Stratford	Thiepval Memorial	Attack on Longueval
19/07/1916	Darlington, Richard	Pte	18618	Hackney	Thiepval Memorial	Attack on Longueval
19/07/1916	Davies, Daniel George	Pte	12880	Hull	Thiepval Memorial	Attack on Longueval
19/07/1916	Dixon, Arthur	A/Sgt	12408	Greets Grn	Thiepval Memorial	Attack on Longueval
19/07/1916	Dixon, Charles Henry	Pte	12275	Birmingham	Thiepval Memorial	Attack on Longueval
19/07/1916	Dyke, Percy	L/Cpl	17923	Devizes	Sucrerie Brit Cem	Attack on Longueval
19/07/1916	Few, Herbert Leonard	Pte	12877	Earley	Thiepval Memorial	Attack on Longueval
19/07/1916	Freeman, Albert	Pte	13219	Bethnal Grn	Thiepval Memorial	Attack on Longueval
19/07/1916	Grosvenor, William	A/CSM	10157	Wolverhampton	Thiepval Memorial	Attack on Longueval
19/07/1916	Haycock, Charles	A/Cpl	12312	Wolverhampton	Thiepval Memorial	Attack on Longueval
19/07/1916	Head, Frank William	L/Cpl	25236	Guildford	Thiepval Memorial	Attack on Longueval
19/07/1916	Headington, Frank	Pte	12860	Easthampstead	Thiepval Memorial	Attack on Longueval
19/07/1916	Hunt, Frank	Pte	12709	Brixton	Thiepval Memorial	Attack on Longueval
19/07/1916	Jenkins, Arthur	Pte	12789	Bracknell	Thiepval Memorial	Attack on Longueval
19/07/1916	Jenkins, Frederick Albert	A/Sgt	12913	Bow	Thiepval Memorial	Attack on Longueval
19/07/1916	Johnson, Samuel Robert	Pte	12478	Battersea	Thiepval Memorial	Attack on Longueval
19/07/1916	Knight, Frederick	Pte	17468	Millwall	Thiepval Memorial	Attack on Longueval
19/07/1916	Lynch, Patrick	A/Sgt	12508	Rotherhythe	Thiepval Memorial	Attack on Longueval
19/07/1916	Moore, Edward	Pte	15369	Walworth	Thiepval Memorial	Attack on Longueval
19/07/1916	Muir, John Wallace	Pte	12696	Kidderminster	Thiepval Memorial	Attack on Longueval
19/07/1916	Poulter, Sidney	Pte	15337	Swallowfield	Thiepval Memorial	Attack on Longueval
19/07/1916	Pusey, James Edward	Pte	12821	Chalvey	Delville Wood Cem	Attack on Longueval
19/07/1916	Roberts, Robert	Pte	16392	Hurst	Serre Road No 2 Cem	Attack on Longueval
19/07/1916	Rylands, Alfred	Pte	12093	Canning Town	Thiepval Memorial	Attack on Longueval
19/07/1916	Thomson, Jack	Pte	12024	Holbourne	Thiepval Memorial	Attack on Longueval
19/07/1916	Todd, William Walter	L/Cpl	12182	Walthamstow	Thiepval Memorial	Attack on Longueval
19/07/1916	Walker, Arthur	L/Cpl	12085	Regents Pk	Thiepval Memorial	Attack on Longueval
19/07/1916	Wilkins, Henry John	Pte	12865	Reading	Thiepval Memorial	Attack on Longueval
19/07/1916	Witcher, Joseph Arthur	Pte	12201	London	Thiepval Memorial	Attack on Longueval
19/07/1916	Wootton, Alfred Edward	L/Cpl	12319	Wednesbury	Bray Military Cem	Attack on Longueval

Date	Name	Rank	Number	Birthplace	Cemetery name	Battalion location
20/07/1916	Collier, Samuel Robert	2/Lieut			Thiepval Memorial	Delville Wood
20/07/1916	Godfrey, John James	Pte	12142	Hackney	Thiepval Memorial	Delville Wood
06/08/1916	Cooper, Walter Francis	Pte	20124	Yardley Wood	Ploegsteert Memorial	Estaires
11/08/1916	Dennis, Edward	Pte	25256	Overstrand	Croix-du-Bac Brit Cem	La Boudrelle
17/08/1916	Rogers, Edward Joseph	Sgt	10372	Reading	Thiepval Memorial	Bailleul
27/09/1916	Highton, Thomas	L/Cpl	25264	Stratford	Thiepval Memorial	Thiepval
27/09/1916	Pratt, Reginald	Pte	36425		Thiepval Memorial	Thiepval
28/09/1916	Lambert, Horace Edward	Pte	36585	Gooderstone	Thiepval Memorial	Thiepval
28/09/1916	Nobbs, Herbert	Pte	36601	March	Thiepval Memorial	Thiepval
29/09/1916	Adams, Frederick William	Pte	36523	Cambridge	Mill Road Cemetery	Thiepval
29/09/1916	Badrick, George	Pte	36256		Thiepval Memorial	Thiepval
29/09/1916	Grimsdale, Charles Arthur	Pte	19024	Little Hamden	Regina Trench Cem	Thiepval
29/09/1916	Hemeley, Gordon Victor	Pte	36334	Berkhamsted	Thiepval Memorial	Thiepval
29/09/1916	Matthews, Thomas	Pte	36593	London	Mill Road Cemetery	Thiepval
29/09/1916	Mew, Arthur Henry	L/Cpl	17748	Nettlebed	Thiepval Memorial	Thiepval
29/09/1916	Mumford, Albert Henry	A/Cpl	16498	West Bromwich	Thiepval Memorial	Thiepval
29/09/1916	Perrin, Obadiah	Pte	36607		Mill Road Cemetery	Thiepval
29/09/1916	Presland, John	Pte	36418		Thiepval Memorial	Thiepval
29/09/1916	Wilson, George Herbert	Pte	39400	Peckham	Mill Road Cemetery	Thiepval
30/09/1916	Aldridge, John Alfred	Pte	36234		Thiepval Memorial	Thiepval
30/09/1916	Angell, Francis Thomas	Pte	36230		Thiepval Memorial	Thiepval
30/09/1916	Bebee, Alexander Denman	2/Lieut			Blighty Valley Cemetery	Thiepval
30/09/1916	Drake, William John	Pte	36302		Thiepval Memorial	Thiepval
30/09/1916	Felton, Godfrey	Pte	36309		Thiepval Memorial	Thiepval
30/09/1916	Gough, Frank	Cpl	12656	Aston	Thiepval Memorial	Thiepval
30/09/1916	Hughes, Frederick Henry	Pte	12912	Bermondsey	Regina Trench Cem	Thiepval
30/09/1916	Huxtable, Harry	Pte	22800	Lancaster	Thiepval Memorial	Thiepval
30/09/1916	Rossiter, James	Pte	36444	Hertford	Thiepval Memorial	Thiepval
30/09/1916	Southall, Thomas James	Pte	39366	Wordesley	Regina Trench Cem	Thiepval
30/09/1916	Talbot, William	Pte	12307	Handsworth	Thiepval Memorial	Thiepval
30/09/1916	Wren, Josiah	Pte	36503		Thiepval Memorial	Thiepval
01/10/1916	Freeman, George Cyril	Capt			Blighty Valley Cemetery	Thiepval
01/10/1916	Slater, Howard Joseph	Pte	36449		Thiepval Memorial	Thiepval
01/10/1916	Stagg, Harry	Pte	36476		Thiepval Memorial	Thiepval
01/10/1916	Turney, Edward Charles	Pte	36482		Thiepval Memorial	Thiepval
02/10/1916	Carter, Charles	Pte	36287		Thiepval Memorial	Schwaben Redoubt
02/10/1916	Chalkley, George	Pte	16279		Serre Road No 2 Cem	Schwaben Redoubt
02/10/1916	Dale, Thomas George	Pte	21589	Bray	Thiepval Memorial	Schwaben Redoubt
02/10/1916	Game, William	Pte	36328	Hertford	Thiepval Memorial	Schwaben Redoubt
02/10/1916	Gray, John	Pte	36317	Hitchin	Thiepval Memorial	Schwaben Redoubt
02/10/1916	Ravenor, Geoffrey Paxton	2/Lieut			Blighty Valley Cemetery	Schwaben Redoubt
02/10/1916	Woodhouse, Frederick	A/CQMS	12989	Southsea	Blighty Valley Cemetery	Schwaben Redoubt
03/10/1916	Cooper, Frederick	A/Cpl	16037	Reading	Thiepval Memorial	Schwaben Redoubt
03/10/1916	Davis, Arthur John	L/Cpl	12848	Sutton Courtenay	Thiepval Memorial	Schwaben Redoubt
03/10/1916	Hearn, Claude	Sgt	10248	Woodley	Bray Vale Brit Cem	Schwaben Redoubt
03/10/1916	Wakelin, Albert George	Pte	36495		Grandcourt Rd Cemetery	Schwaben Redoubt
04/10/1916	Allen, Tom	Pte	36231		Villers-Bretonneux Mil Cem	Schwaben Redoubt
05/10/1916	Ansell, William	L/Cpl	12824	Sonning	Thiepval Memorial	Hédauville
05/10/1916	Crombie-Rodgers, David George	Pte	36443		Thiepval Memorial	Hédauville
05/10/1916	Dodds, Reginald John	Pte	36893	Conesly	Bray Vale Brit Cem	Hédauville
05/10/1916	Malkin, Francis Henry	Pte	36390		Regina Trench Cem	Hédauville
05/10/1916	May, Walter	L/Cpl	12760	Reading	Thiepval Memorial	Hédauville
10/10/1916	Russell, George Frederick	Pte	12556	Birmingham	Albert Communal Cemetery Ext	Boisbergues
17/10/1916	Allen, Hugh	Pte	36524	Elm	Thiepval Memorial	Albert
17/10/1916	Allgood, Harry	Pte	36522	Coton	Thiepval Memorial	Albert
17/10/1916	Dowie, William James	Pte	36959	Grimsby	Thiepval Memorial	Albert
17/10/1916	Lawrence, Thomas	Pte	36387	Hertford	Thiepval Memorial	Albert
17/10/1916	Manser, William	Pte	36395		Thiepval Memorial	Albert
19/10/1916	Bunce, Arthur	Pte	39367	Winchester	Courcelette Brit Cem	Albert
19/10/1916	Diver, Frederick William	Pte	36551	Hadenham	Thiepval Memorial	Albert
19/10/1916	Phipps, Arthur	Pte	19644	Abingdon	Thiepval Memorial	Albert
20/10/1916	Bushnell, John William	Pte	19660	Feltham	Thiepval Memorial	Regina Trench
21/10/1916	Taylor, Sidney Maurice	Pte	26346	Reading	Thiepval Memorial	Albert
24/10/1916	White, Charles William	Pte	12838	Hayes	Thiepval Memorial	In line Mocquet Farm
30/10/1916	Puncher, Frank	Pte	36429		Courcelette Brit Cem	Reserve Mocquet Farm
31/10/1916	Johnson, Henry Alfred	Pte	36369		Thiepval Memorial	Reserve Mocquet Farm
01/11/1916	Ivory, George	Pte	36264	Dunstable	Regina Trench Cem	Regina Trench
11/11/1916	Dawes, Arthur	Pte	36292		Thiepval Memorial	Regina Trench
12/11/1916	Deville, Ramah	Pte	36301		Stump Road Cem	Regina Trench
12/11/1916	Lawrence, Herbert Alfred	Pte	36380		Thiepval Memorial	Regina Trench
12/11/1916	Ringsell, Edwin	L/Cpl	36447		Thiepval Memorial	Regina Trench
12/11/1916	Smith, George William	L/Cpl	10310	Hungerford	Thiepval Memorial	Regina Trench

Died of wounds

Date	Name	Rank	Number	Birthplace	Cemetery name
05/10/1916	Atkins, Bernard Owen	Pte	36226		Puchevillers Brit Cem
02/10/1916	Baker, Albert James	Pte	12724	East Barnet	Daours Comm Cem Ext
20/07/1916	Brown, George Harry	Pte	11332	South Godstone	Corbie Comm Cem Ext
29/09/1916	Burrows, Walter	Pte	36887	Croxton Kerrial	Puchevillers Brit Cem
08/10/1916	Cakebread, Ernest	Pte	36276		Holy Trinity Bengeo
15/10/1916	Cambray, Edwin	Pte	26363	Pangbourne	Warloy Baillon Comm Cem Ext
21/04/1916	Clarke, Edward	Pte	12571	St Pancras	La Neuville Comm Cem
21/07/1916	Collins, Thomas	Pte	25241	Reepham	Corbie Comm Cem Ext
02/07/1916	Cook, Alexander Thomas	Sgt	10130	Clerkenwell	La Neuville Brit Cem

Date	Name	Rank	Number	Birthplace	Cemetery name
28/03/1916	Coombes, James	Pte	12594	Baptist Mills	Corbie Comm Cem
02/07/1916	Cordell, Albert Victor	Pte	12933	Stratford	La Neuville Brit Cem
05/10/1916	Cullum, Tom	Pte	36891	Grimsby	Borough of Grimsby Cemetery
02/07/1916	Danby, Sam	Pte	16068	Bewdley	Heilly Station Cemetery
05/07/1916	Day, Arthur Albert	Pte	12420	Birmingham	Boisguillaume Comm Cem
27/04/1916	Dean, Walter Charles	Pte	12849	Eastbury	St Sever Cem
03/10/1916	Dymoke, Walter George	2/Lieut			Contay Brit Cem
02/07/1916	Earle, Christopher	Cpl	12845	Leatherhead	Thiepval Memorial
01/07/1916	Eaton, George	Pte	16670	Newbury	La Neuville Brit Cem
19/10/1916	Field, Cornelius	Pte	17339	Tidal Basin Essex	Pozières Brit Cem
06/09/1916	Freeman, Harold Sidney	Pte	11324	Greenham	Newbury Old Cemetery
22/07/1916	Fuller, Cyril John	2/Lieut			Dive Copse Brit Cem
25/07/1916	Glen, Andrew	Sgt	12445	Grangemouth	Grandsable Cemetery
01/07/1916	Gridley, George	Pte	12500	Camberwell	Dive Copse Brit Cem
21/10/1916	Groom, Herbert	Pte	36319		St Marys Hatfield
02/10/1916	Hudson (Huson?), John William	Pte	36354	Hertford	Puchevillers Brit Cem
14/07/1916	Humphrey, Charles Percival	Sgt	12651	Camberwell	Abbeville Communal Cemetery
23/07/1916	Hutton, Alfred William	Pte	19676	Brentford	Corbie Comm Cem Ext
02/10/1916	Inett, Ernest Frank	Pte	12393	Birmingham	Puchevillers Brit Cem
13/07/1916	Lankford, Edward James	Pte	25238	Deal	St Sever Cem
26/10/1916	Lipcombe, Oliver Percy	A/Cpl	17322	Bray	Boulogne Eastern Cemetery
02/07/1916	London, Frederick Charles	L/Cpl	12527	Battersea	La Neuville Brit Cem
17/07/1916	McLean, John Victor	2/Lieut			Golders Green Crematorium
09/07/1916	Mosely, Albert	Pte	12239	Birmingham	Abbeville Communal Cemetery
07/10/1916	Neale, Maurice	Pte	23803	Watford	St Sever Cem
05/04/1916	Newman, Alfred	Pte	12265	Birmingham	Birmingham (Handsworth) Cemetery
12/07/1916	Nicholls, James	Pte	10064	Wallingford	Boulogne Eastern Cemetery
02/10/1916	Norden, Frederick John	Pte	36600	W Wratting	Mont Huon Mil Cem
03/10/1916	Peak, James	L/Cpl	12286	Leicester	Puchevillers Brit Cem
01/10/1916	Pearson, George	Pte	6926	Baston	Puchevillers Brit Cem
01/07/1916	Perkins, Frederick George	L/Cpl	12719	Camberwell	La Neuville Comm Cem
27/07/1916	Pettifer, Arthur	Pte	12576	Shefford	Campton and Shefford Cemetery
07/07/1916	Phillips, Albert	Pte	13946	Tottenham	Etaples Mil Cem
29/09/1916	Randall, Ernest Arthur	Pte	22821	Reading	Varennes Mil Cem
27/07/1916	Ricketts, Frederick James	Pte	12779	Buckham	Corbie Comm Cem Ext
02/07/1916	Rising, William Thomas	Pte	12948	Fulham	La Neuville Brit Cem
01/07/1916	Rogers, George	Pte	12135	Stepney	La Neuville Brit Cem
08/10/1916	Rudd, Leonard John	Pte	36436		Puchevillers Brit Cem
19/07/1916	Sadler, Hereward Patterson	2/Lieut			Carnoy Military Cem
11/07/1916	Saye, Lancelot Hugo	2/Lieut			Etaples Mil Cem
10/10/1916	Sear, William	Pte	36470		Chichester Cemetery
23/07/1916	Stieber, Frederick Richard	Sgt	10128	Reading	Abbeville Communal Cemetery
14/09/1916	Stride, John James	Pte	12581	Tipton	Oldbury Cemetery
18/07/1916	Tegg, Edmund Annanias	Sgt	12853	Reading	Hollybrook Mem Southampton
14/11/1916	Tew, Wilfred Henry	Pte	36486		Contay Brit Cem
29/03/1916	Thompson, George Stanley	L/Cpl	12253	Ruardene	Corbie Comm Cem
26/07/1916	Turnbull, Thomas	A/Cpl	16355	St Hilda	Netley Military Cemetery
15/10/1916	Warner, James	Pte	36511		Contay Brit Cem
16/10/1916	Webb, George	Pte	36513	Watford	Contay Brit Cem
01/07/1916	Webber, Stephen John	Pte	12725	Islington	Daours Comm Cem Ext
29/09/1916	Welling, Walter	Pte	36502	Berkhamsted	Warloy Baillon Comm Cem Ext
21/07/1916	Whadcoat, Ernest William	Pte	12193	Camberwell	La Neuville Brit Cem
02/07/1916	Wheeler, George	Pte	12711	Bermondsey	Carnoy Military Cem
29/09/1916	Wick, Francis	Pte	36519		Warloy Baillon Comm Cem Ext
10/10/1916	Wren, John	Pte	36506	Widford	Mont Huon Mil Cem
15/10/1916	Wright, Herbert	Pte	36479	St Albans	Contay Brit Cem

8th Battalion

Killed in action

Date	Name	Rank	Number	Birthplace	Cemetery name	Battalion location
15/10/1916	Wright, Herbert	Pte	36479	St Albans	Contay Brit Cem	
02/02/1916	Threlfall, William	Pte	37051	Chorley	Thiepval Memorial	Allouagne
09/02/1916	Thurmer, Edward Charles	L/Cpl	17228	Winkfield	Thiepval Memorial	Allouagne
20/02/1916	Pounds, Albert Alec	Pte	15221	Reading	Maroc Brit Cem	Front line Cité Calonne
21/02/1916	McDermott, John	Pte	18360	Silvertown	Maroc Brit Cem	Front line Cité Calonne
11/03/1916	Houghton, William	L/Cpl	14738	Manchester	St Patricks Cem	Front line near Loos
12/03/1916	Crawford, George	Pte	18813	Norwood	St Patricks Cem	Front line near Loos
18/03/1916	Cox, William Ernest	Pte	18568	Bradfield	Arras Memorial	Front line near Loos
18/03/1916	Heaver, Walter	Pte	17464	Boxford	St Patricks Cem	Front line near Loos
29/03/1916	Mulcock, Walter Harold	L/Cpl	8372	Swindon	Maroc Brit Cem	Billets at Les Brébis
03/04/1916	Massey, William	Pte	14915	Birmingham	Maroc Brit Cem	Maroc Sector
03/04/1916	Walters, Thomas	Pte	19205	Oxford	Maroc Brit Cem	Maroc Sector
19/04/1916	Ward, Sidney Howard	Sgt	9855	Birmingham	Arras Memorial	Maroc Sector
26/04/1916	Brombley, Richard	Pte	14393	Easthampstead	Arras Memorial	Maroc Sector
27/04/1916	Caladine, John Henry	L/Cpl	14373	Sutton	Bully-Grenay Comm Cem Fr Ext	Les Brébis
03/05/1916	Moore, Ernest	Pte	18908	East Grinstead	Arras Memorial	Raid at Double Crassier
03/05/1916	Turner, Henry John	Cpl	13229	Stepney	Maroc Brit Cem	Raid at Double Crassier
04/05/1916	Nobes, William Frank	Cpl	16459	Portsmouth	Arras Memorial	Front line Double Crassier
07/05/1916	Little, Frederick Albert	Pte	18815	Kintbury	Maroc Brit Cem	Front line Double Crassier
27/05/1916	Blake, Frederick Mark	Pte	19147	Knowl Hill	Loos Brit Cem	Under attack at Calonne
27/05/1916	Buckland, Henry John	L/Cpl	18521	Whitley	Loos Brit Cem	Under attack at Calonne

Date	Name	Rank	Number	Birthplace	Cemetery name	Battalion location
27/05/1916	Carter, George Day	Pte	18115	Shoreham	Loos Brit Cem	Under attack at Calonne
27/05/1916	Chadd, Peter	Pte	18163	Brighton	Loos Brit Cem	Under attack at Calonne
27/05/1916	Crouch, Norman Colin Edward	Pte	18053	Droxford	Loos Brit Cem	Under attack at Calonne
27/05/1916	Crumpton, William	Pte	18613	Oldbury	Loos Brit Cem	Under attack at Calonne
27/05/1916	Fairchild, Arthur Henry	Pte	18755	Picketfield	Loos Brit Cem	Under attack at Calonne
27/05/1916	Greenough, George	Pte	15590	Hampstead Norris	Loos Brit Cem	Under attack at Calonne
27/05/1916	Hester, Harry	Pte	17956	Thame	Loos Brit Cem	Under attack at Calonne
27/05/1916	Hopkins, William	Pte	18930	Shaw	Loos Brit Cem	Under attack at Calonne
27/05/1916	Klementaski, Louis Arthur	2/Lieut			Bully-Grenay Comm Cem Br Ext	Under attack at Calonne
27/05/1916	Wiskin, George	Pte	18902	Canning Town	Loos Brit Cem	Under attack at Calonne
13/06/1916	Thomas, William	L/Cpl	13195	Reading	Maroc Brit Cem	Front line Double Crassier
11/07/1916	Snell, Francis Saxon	2/Lieut			Fricourt Brit Cem	Trenches at Lozenge Wood
12/07/1916	Glasse, Michael Joseph	Pte	19037	Newington Butts	Thiepval Memorial	Contalmaison - Mametz
12/07/1916	Pearcey, Edward John	L/Sgt	18932	Rockbourne	Gordon Dump Cemetery	Contalmaison - Mametz
13/07/1916	Charley, Daniel William	Pte	14572	Coventry	Thiepval Memorial	Contalmaison - Mametz
13/07/1916	Connell, Cornelius	Pte	18670	Westminster	Thiepval Memorial	Contalmaison - Mametz
13/07/1916	Gibbs, Charles	Pte	17325	Newbury	Thiepval Memorial	Contalmaison - Mametz
14/07/1916	Allen, Cecil Briggs	Pte	16805	Reading	Thiepval Memorial	Attack at Pearl Alley
14/07/1916	Bosher, Charles	Pte	18164	Harwell	Thiepval Memorial	Attack at Pearl Alley
14/07/1916	Coles, Albert	Pte	17955	Henley	Thiepval Memorial	Attack at Pearl Alley
14/07/1916	Cummins, Hubert Charles	Pte	18684	Newbury	Thiepval Memorial	Attack at Pearl Alley
14/07/1916	Edgington, Reginald Alfred	L/Cpl	20030	Reading	Thiepval Memorial	Attack at Pearl Alley
14/07/1916	Evans, Alfred	Pte	14628	Birmingham	Thiepval Memorial	Attack at Pearl Alley
14/07/1916	Neale, George	Pte	14479	Coventry	Flatiron Copse Cemetery	Attack at Pearl Alley
14/07/1916	Nixon, John	Pte	18928	Clewer	Thiepval Memorial	Attack at Pearl Alley
14/07/1916	Ralph, Frank	Pte	14651	Birmingham	Thiepval Memorial	Attack at Pearl Alley
14/07/1916	Robinson, Arthur James	Pte	20125	Radford	Thiepval Memorial	Attack at Pearl Alley
14/07/1916	Sayer, James William	Pte	16144	Litcham	Gordon Dump Cemetery	Attack at Pearl Alley
22/07/1916	Blackwell, Sidney Harry	Pte	20137	Abingdon	Thiepval Memorial	Support for attack at Martinpuich
22/07/1916	Faulkner, David	Pte	18922	Birmingham	Ovillers Mil Cem	Support for attack at Martinpuich
22/07/1916	Hemming, Joseph	Pte	20138	Abingdon	Ovillers Mil Cem	Support for attack at Martinpuich
23/07/1916	Cooper, Frank	Pte	17968	Hadley	Thiepval Memorial	Front Line Mametz
23/07/1916	Forse, William Henry	Pte	22001	Gloucester	Thiepval Memorial	Front Line Mametz
24/07/1916	Chandler, Walter Albert	Pte	18220	Brixton	Thiepval Memorial	Front Line Mametz
24/07/1916	Cox, Charles Benjamin	Pte	22121	Totterdown	Thiepval Memorial	Front Line Mametz
24/07/1916	Fear, Harry	Pte	22112	Weston Super Mare	Thiepval Memorial	Front Line Mametz
24/07/1916	Hingley, Harry	Pte	14621	Dudley	Thiepval Memorial	Front Line Mametz
24/07/1916	May, Joseph	Pte	13183	Hampstead Marshall	Thiepval Memorial	Front Line Mametz
25/07/1916	Blewett, Reginald	L/Cpl	18875	Mt Charles	Thiepval Memorial	Bivouacs in Baisieux Wood
25/07/1916	Branscombe, Henry	Pte	15529	Egham	Thiepval Memorial	Bivouacs in Baisieux Wood
25/07/1916	Harris, Robert	Pte	19028	Bray	Thiepval Memorial	Bivouacs in Baisieux Wood
25/07/1916	Taylor, William James	Pte	16198	Bray	Thiepval Memorial	Bivouacs in Baisieux Wood
13/08/1916	Conyers, Walter Neville	2/Lieut			Thiepval Memorial	Bécourt
13/08/1916	Harrison, Cecil George Bradford	2/Lieut			Thiepval Memorial	Bécourt
17/08/1916	Brown, William	Pte	14382	Long Wittenham	Thiepval Memorial	Mametz Wood
17/08/1916	Reeves, Alfred	L/Cpl	13311	Wokingham	Thiepval Memorial	Mametz Wood
18/08/1916	Adams, William John	Pte	17981	Longworth	Caterpillar Valley Cem	Attack at Bazentin le Petit
18/08/1916	Bissley, William Howe	2/Lieut			Thiepval Memorial	Attack at Bazentin le Petit
18/08/1916	Broome, Charles George	Pte	18619	Camberley	Caterpillar Valley Cem	Attack at Bazentin le Petit
18/08/1916	Charlton, Lawrence	L/Sgt	18952	Newbury	Caterpillar Valley Cem	Attack at Bazentin le Petit
18/08/1916	Claringbold, Robert	Pte	17973	Portland	Thiepval Memorial	Attack at Bazentin le Petit
18/08/1916	Clements, Charles Henry	Pte	18754	Easthampstead	Thiepval Memorial	Attack at Bazentin le Petit
18/08/1916	Clemie, Edwin	Pte	17964	Westbourne Pk	Thiepval Memorial	Attack at Bazentin le Petit
18/08/1916	Davies, William	Pte	18994	Llanelly	Thiepval Memorial	Attack at Bazentin le Petit
18/08/1916	Davis, Joseph	Pte	21652	Hendred	Thiepval Memorial	Attack at Bazentin le Petit
18/08/1916	Groves, Leonard	Pte	18912	Datchet	Thiepval Memorial	Attack at Bazentin le Petit
18/08/1916	Hawksbee, Edward Walter	Pte	18881	Bethnal Grn	Thiepval Memorial	Attack at Bazentin le Petit
18/08/1916	Herne, Alfred	L/Cpl	18869	Clewer	Thiepval Memorial	Attack at Bazentin le Petit
18/08/1916	Hickman, Thomas William	Pte	21861	Kenilworth	Thiepval Memorial	Attack at Bazentin le Petit
18/08/1916	Hook, Albert James	Pte	21549	Abingdon	Thiepval Memorial	Attack at Bazentin le Petit
18/08/1916	Howett, Charles	Pte	21579	Norwich	Thiepval Memorial	Attack at Bazentin le Petit
18/08/1916	Hunt, Jack	Pte	19467	Aston Hill	Thiepval Memorial	Attack at Bazentin le Petit
18/08/1916	Joyce, Fred	L/Cpl	21543	Compton	Thiepval Memorial	Attack at Bazentin le Petit
18/08/1916	Keenan, Owen	Pte	18882	Oxford	Thiepval Memorial	Attack at Bazentin le Petit
18/08/1916	Mitchener, Sidney James	Pte	18621	Silvertown	Thiepval Memorial	Attack at Bazentin le Petit
18/08/1916	Paford, John	Pte	17158	Poplar	Thiepval Memorial	Attack at Bazentin le Petit
18/08/1916	Phillips, David	Pte	15489	Briton Ferry	Thiepval Memorial	Attack at Bazentin le Petit
18/08/1916	Pike, Sidney William	Pte	17447	Mile End	Thiepval Memorial	Attack at Bazentin le Petit
18/08/1916	Pill, Arthur	Pte	21551	Shillingford	Thiepval Memorial	Attack at Bazentin le Petit
18/08/1916	Pritchard, Thomas	Pte	21713	Woodcote	Thiepval Memorial	Attack at Bazentin le Petit
18/08/1916	Rogers, Albert Victor	Pte	21774	Chertsey	Thiepval Memorial	Attack at Bazentin le Petit
18/08/1916	Taylor, Arthur George	Pte	21754	Reading	Thiepval Memorial	Attack at Bazentin le Petit
18/08/1916	Taylor, Frederick	Pte	22257	Newbold on Avon	Thiepval Memorial	Attack at Bazentin le Petit
18/08/1916	Thomas, Sidney Charles	Pte	21537	Whiteley	Thiepval Memorial	Attack at Bazentin le Petit
18/08/1916	Timms, Tom	Pte	17997	Stanford	Flatiron Copse Cemetery	Attack at Bazentin le Petit
18/08/1916	Tridgett, Frederick Charles	Pte	12169	Chigwell Row	Thiepval Memorial	Attack at Bazentin le Petit
18/08/1916	Wiggins, George	Pte	21587	Reading	Thiepval Memorial	Attack at Bazentin le Petit
18/08/1916	Young, William	Pte	21775	Benson	Thiepval Memorial	Attack at Bazentin le Petit
19/08/1916	Fisher, Arthur	L/Cpl	16516	St Helens	Thiepval Memorial	Front line Mametz Wood
19/08/1916	Joy, Edward Sydney	2/Lieut			Caterpillar Valley Cem	Front line Mametz Wood
19/08/1916	Peacock, Harold	Pte	13856	Sittingbourne	Thiepval Memorial	Front line Mametz Wood
19/08/1916	Potter, Frank	Pte	13926	Finsbury	Thiepval Memorial	Front line Mametz Wood
20/08/1916	Fergusson, Ralph	Pte	18129	Leith		Support trenches Mametz Wood
21/08/1916	Hill, Arthur Paul	L/Cpl	14121	Battersea	Thiepval Memorial	Support trenches Mametz Wood
27/08/1916	Smart, George	Pte	18100	Newbury	Thiepval Memorial	Support trenches Mametz Wood
27/08/1916	Wickens, Gerald Lionel	Pte	18276	Shilton	Thiepval Memorial	Support trenches Mametz Wood

Date	Name	Rank	Number	Birthplace	Cemetery name	Battalion location
28/08/1916	Rowney, John Frederick	Cpl	13274	Islington	Flatiron Copse Cemetery	Support trenches Mametz Wood
29/08/1916	Wilson, Thomas	Pte	16544	Ramsbury	Chapelle Brit Cem	High Wood
30/08/1916	Maslin, William Frank	Pte	16638	Reading	Thiepval Memorial	Support trenches Mametz Wood
31/08/1916	Hedge, Frederick Owen	L/Cpl	25247	Westminster	Thiepval Memorial	Support trenches Mametz Wood
31/08/1916	Poman, Francis Richard	Pte	22118	Newtown	Thiepval Memorial	Support trenches Mametz Wood
31/08/1916	Poole, Alfred Charles	Pte	22089	Weston on Bath	Thiepval Memorial	Support trenches Mametz Wood
31/08/1916	Rich, Reginald	Pte	21858	Bedminster	Thiepval Memorial	Support trenches Mametz Wood
01/09/1916	Folley, Walter George	Sgt	14869	Cookham	Flatiron Copse Cemetery	Support trenches Mametz Wood
01/09/1916	Swindon, George	Sgt	14719	Smethwick	Thiepval Memorial	Support trenches Mametz Wood
01/09/1916	Wort, Thomas	Cpl	14954	Birmingham	Flatiron Copse Cemetery	Support trenches Mametz Wood
03/09/1916	Beckett, James Harold	Pte	21582	Birmingham	Thiepval Memorial	Attack at High Wood
03/09/1916	Boniface, James	Pte	21021	Bognor	Thiepval Memorial	Attack at High Wood
03/09/1916	Budden, Sidney	A/Cpl	18334	Winterbourne	Caterpillar Valley Cem	Attack at High Wood
03/09/1916	Butt, William Frederick	Pte	14228	Barnards Grn	Thiepval Memorial	Attack at High Wood
03/09/1916	Chambers, Cleveland Hugh	2/Lieut			London Cemetery	Attack at High Wood
03/09/1916	Cook, Frederick George	Pte	17752	Lambeth	Thiepval Memorial	Attack at High Wood
03/09/1916	Davis, Sydney Charles	Pte	19972	Olney	Caterpillar Valley Cem	Attack at High Wood
03/09/1916	Dickson, Sydney	Pte	13287	Tunbridge Wells	Caterpillar Valley Cem	Attack at High Wood
03/09/1916	Doran, Harry	Pte	18786	Reading	Caterpillar Valley Cem	Attack at High Wood
03/09/1916	Edens, Lionel George	2/Lieut			Thistle Dump Cemetery	Attack at High Wood
03/09/1916	Ellis, Edgar Pens	Pte	17961	Poplar	Caterpillar Valley Cem	Attack at High Wood
03/09/1916	Emery, Thomas	Pte	18142	Reading	Caterpillar Valley Cem	Attack at High Wood
03/09/1916	Gregory, Thomas Reddington	Pte	21857	Sutton in Ashfield	Thistle Dump Cemetery	Attack at High Wood
03/09/1916	Hobro, Alfred Ernest	Pte	21018	Birmingham	Caterpillar Valley Cem	Attack at High Wood
03/09/1916	Holmes, Charles Leonard	Pte	19989	Reading	Thiepval Memorial	Attack at High Wood
03/09/1916	Hosier, Heber John	Pte	17980	Abingdon	Thiepval Memorial	Attack at High Wood
03/09/1916	Jones, Harry	Pte	22244	Reading	Thiepval Memorial	Attack at High Wood
03/09/1916	Langton, Ernest Charles	Pte	13533	Woodford	Thiepval Memorial	Attack at High Wood
03/09/1916	Mareham (or Marcham), James	Pte	13122	Reading	Thiepval Memorial	Attack at High Wood
03/09/1916	Mead, Charles	Pte	18500	Kensington	Thistle Dump Cemetery	Attack at High Wood
03/09/1916	Middleton, William Edward	L/Sgt	18208	Canning Town	Caterpillar Valley Cem	Attack at High Wood
03/09/1916	Morecombe, George	Pte	17287	Lambeth	Caterpillar Valley Cem	Attack at High Wood
03/09/1916	Palmer, Wilfred Percy	Pte	18778	Streatham	Caterpillar Valley Cem	Attack at High Wood
03/09/1916	Pickrell, Henry Bertram	Cpl	39378	Wandsworth	Thiepval Memorial	Attack at High Wood
03/09/1916	Piggott, Richard Harry	Pte	21758	Weybridge	Caterpillar Valley Cem	Attack at High Wood
03/09/1916	Porter, William George	Pte	21763	Reading	Caterpillar Valley Cem	Attack at High Wood
03/09/1916	Prout, Douglas William	2/Lieut			Thiepval Memorial	Attack at High Wood
03/09/1916	Rapley, George Henry	Pte	18748	Binfield	Thiepval Memorial	Attack at High Wood
03/09/1916	Scull, Walter Harvey	Pte	18886	Faccombe	Thiepval Memorial	Attack at High Wood
03/09/1916	Sheppard, Alfred	Pte	22086	Bedminster	Caterpillar Valley Cem	Attack at High Wood
03/09/1916	Smith, George	Pte	18656	Shepherds Bush	Thiepval Memorial	Attack at High Wood
03/09/1916	Stevens, Frank	Pte	21132	Little Bookham	Caterpillar Valley Cem	Attack at High Wood
03/09/1916	Thomas, Benjamin	Pte	19142	Cliften Hampden	London Cemetery	Attack at High Wood
03/09/1916	Titchener, Thomas	L/Cpl	16940	Grove	Thiepval Memorial	Attack at High Wood
03/09/1916	Wallace, Frank	Pte	20155	Letcombe Regis	Thiepval Memorial	Attack at High Wood
03/09/1916	Widdick, James	Pte	15504	Speen	Thistle Dump Cemetery	Attack at High Wood
19/09/1916	Evans, Walter Thomas	Cpl	13895	Kingsland	Thistle Dump Cemetery	Bazentin le Grand
22/09/1916	Burgess, Henry	Pte	36999	Ashton on Mersey	Thiepval Memorial	Trenches E of High Wood
22/09/1916	Lewis, Herbert John	Pte	36858	Tugwarden	Caterpillar Valley Cem	Trenches E of High Wood
22/09/1916	Shackell, Frederick Charles	Pte	36784	Worcester	Caterpillar Valley Cem	Trenches E of High Wood
22/09/1916	Southwell, Enos	Pte	36867	Southampton	Thiepval Memorial	Trenches E of High Wood
23/09/1916	Clarke, Philip Christian Campbell	Cpl	13238	Gillingham	Thiepval Memorial	Trenches E of High Wood
23/09/1916	Daw, Albert James	Sgt	36640	Leominster	Thiepval Memorial	Trenches E of High Wood
23/09/1916	Jones, Frank	Cpl	14182	Cranborne	Thiepval Memorial	Trenches E of High Wood
24/09/1916	Partington, Ralph Walter	Pte	37038	Bolton	Thiepval Memorial	Bazentin le Grand
24/09/1916	Wilkinson, Frank	Pte	37174	Halton	Thiepval Memorial	Bazentin le Grand
23/10/1916	Hales, William Clifford	2/Lieut			Bancourt British Cem	Franleu
02/12/1916	Greenaway, Alfred Charles	Pte	18227	Ipsden	Thiepval Memorial	Front line nr Warlincourt
02/12/1916	Watton, Charles	Pte	36705	Ridgeway	Thiepval Memorial	Front line nr Warlincourt
03/12/1916	Giles, George William	Pte	20157	Wallingford	Thiepval Memorial	Front line nr Warlincourt
03/12/1916	Nash, Samuel	L/Cpl	8930	London	Thiepval Memorial	Front line nr Warlincourt
03/12/1916	Walton, William	Pte	39396	Kitlington	Thiepval Memorial	Front line nr Warlincourt
03/12/1916	Whittle, George Thomas	Pte	36984	Bolton	Thiepval Memorial	Front line nr Warlincourt
04/12/1916	Bennett, Walter	L/Sgt	13082	Hurley	Thiepval Memorial	Front line nr Warlincourt
04/12/1916	Bowler, Peter	Cpl	17814	Denham	Thiepval Memorial	Front line nr Warlincourt
04/12/1916	Kirkby, Henry Horatio	Pte	18530	North Fleet	Thiepval Memorial	Front line nr Warlincourt
04/12/1916	Lloyd, Thomas	Pte	37117	Denby	Thiepval Memorial	Front line nr Warlincourt
21/12/1916	Minshall, Samuel John	Pte	15006	Rugeley	Thiepval Memorial	Huts at Bazentin le Petit
28/12/1916	Fox, Thomas Sheppard	Pte	36883	Bristol	Thiepval Memorial	In support line Flers
30/12/1916	Bone, Albert Edward	Pte	36748	Odiham	Thiepval Memorial	Camp No 4 Bazentin le Petit
30/12/1916	Payne, Edward George	Pte	18204	Canning Town	Thiepval Memorial	Camp No 4 Bazentin le Petit
30/12/1916	Phillips, Henry	Pte	36750	Selbourne	Thiepval Memorial	Camp No 4 Bazentin le Petit
30/12/1916	Witts, Bertie Henry	L/Cpl	36849	Whitchurch	Thiepval Memorial	Camp No 4 Bazentin le Petit

Died of wounds

Date	Name	Rank	Number	Birthplace	Cemetery name
14/04/1916	Akehurst, Richard	Pte	18289	Paddington	Béthune Town Cem
19/08/1916	Alley, Leslie Thomas	Pte	20162	Birmingham	Dantzig Alley Brit Cem
12/09/1916	Andrews, John	Pte	21578	Warwick	Birmingham (Lodge Hill) Cemetery
13/07/1916	Appleton, Frederick	L/Cpl	13100	Blewbury	Heilly Station Cemetery
14/07/1916	Baker, Thomas Wickens	Pte	20156	Maida Vale	Heilly Station Cemetery
01/09/1916	Banning, John	Pte	14895	Birmingham	Heilly Station Cemetery
05/09/1916	Barnard, Thomas Alfred	Pte	18467	Walworth	Heilly Station Cemetery
01/06/1916	Barrow, James	Lt/QM			Noeux-les-Mines Comm Cem
12/07/1916	Bassett, Arthur James	Pte	14055	Walthamstowe	Thiepval Memorial

Date	Name	Rank	Number	Birthplace	Cemetery name
01/06/1916	Baul, Frederick Charles	Pte	15595	Compton	Noeux-les-Mines Comm Cem
04/12/1916	Beasley, Thomas	Pte	16415	Donnington	Warlencourt Brit Cem
30/08/1916	Blake, William John	Pte	21538	Wantage	Millencourt Comm Cem Ext
01/06/1916	Brown, Arthur	Sgt	14865	Castleford	Noeux-les-Mines Comm Cem
29/03/1916	Brown, Frank Herbert	Pte	17295	Plaistow	Maroc Brit Cem
01/06/1916	Butler, Jack Wilfred	Pte	16467		Noeux-les-Mines Comm Cem
26/07/1916	Clarke, Frederick Wallace	Pte	17930	Whitchurch	St Sever Cem
19/08/1916	Clayton, George Henry	Pte	13687	Wakefield	Dantzig Alley Brit Cem
19/07/1916	Collins, Albert Richard	Pte	18629	Ardington	Boulogne Eastern Cemetery
24/04/1916	Cornish, George Phillip	L/Cpl	18172	Hammersmith	Béthune Town Cem
13/07/1916	Cox, Francis William	Pte	18483	Appleton	Warloy Baillon Comm Cem Ext
18/03/1916	Cresswell, Job	Pte	14889	West Bromwich	Noeux-les-Mines Comm Cem
05/04/1916	Ditton, Kenneth Benedict	Pte	19243	Cookham	Béthune Town Cem
10/03/1916	Dowdell, John	Pte	15520	Vernham Rowe	St Patricks Cem
18/03/1916	Duesbury, John Trevor	L/Cpl	17901	Duffield	Derby Cemetery
06/12/1916	Farley, Albert George	Pte	36725	Aston	Dernancourt Comm Cem Ext
21/02/1916	Foley, George	Pte	13647	Lambeth	Bully-Grenay Comm Cem Fr Ext
28/07/1916	Fudge, Stanley Alfred	A/Sgt	10089	Bath	Daours Comm Cem Ext
22/08/1916	Godding, Benjamin	Pte	21547	Letcombe Regis	Heilly Station Cemetery
28/05/1916	Goulding (Golding), Leonard Francis	L/Cpl	18261	East Hendred	Noeux-les-Mines Comm Cem
18/08/1916	Gregory, William George	Pte	19675	Paddington	Thiepval Memorial
01/01/1916	Gurton, Walter John	L/Cpl	13340	Buckhurst Hill	Dud Corner Cem
03/12/1916	Gwilt, John	Pte	37095	Tipton	Thiepval Memorial
13/03/1916	Harding, Reginald	Pte	18160	Denham Norfolk	Béthune Town Cem
03/12/1916	Harrington, James	Pte	36659	Stourbridge	Bécourt Military Cem
21/05/1916	Harrison, William	Pte	18839	Hounslow	Noeux-les-Mines Comm Cem
19/08/1916	Harriss, Ernest Herbert	Pte	13197	Reading	Thiepval Memorial
21/08/1916	Hayes, Charles	Pte	22087	Bristol	Heilly Station Cemetery
03/12/1916	Hill, William Norman	L/Cpl	37098	Wigan	Warlencourt Brit Cem
20/08/1916	Holland, Henry William	Pte	21804S	Sandhurst	Heilly Station Cemetery
19/10/1916	Hollis, Alfred	Pte	21113	Birmingham	Birmingham (Yardley) Cemetery
21/09/1916	Holmes, Harry Sidney	Cpl	16132	Cold Ash	Newbury Municipal Cem
06/12/1916	Howlett, Sam	Pte	17577	Thame	Dernancourt Comm Cem Ext
26/09/1916	Jones, Herbert Francis Edward	Pte	13598	Bray	Dernancourt Comm Cem Ext
22/08/1916	Kirk, William	Pte	13573	Chelsea	Etaples Mil Cem
28/08/1916	Langley, Frank	L/Cpl	18264	Gt Marlow	Heilly Station Cemetery
01/05/1916	Leatt, Tom	L/Cpl	17932	Skipton	Le Tréport Mil Cem
18/07/1916	Leveridge, Edward	Pte	18004	Lambeth	St Sever Cem
14/07/1916	Maggs, George Ernest	2/Lieut			Dernancourt Comm Cem
12/07/1916	Maskell, George	Pte	17462	West Ilsley	Gordon Dump Cemetery
28/08/1916	Mills, George	Pte	18241	Swinbrook	Millencourt Comm Cem Ext
19/12/1916	Mott, Frederick	L/Sgt	20104	Mottingham	Dernancourt Comm Cem Ext
24/02/1916	Ostler, George Frank	Cpl	18392	Yeovil	Lapugnoy Mil Cem
25/07/1916	Parsons, Harry	Pte	20012	Reading	Abbeville Communal Cemetery
26/09/1916	Parsons, Henry Hodges	Pte	21133	Tidmarsh	Millencourt Comm Cem Ext
21/09/1916	Pearce, Walter Frank	Pte	19987	Reading	Port-de-Paris Cem
02/09/1916	Pillow, Samuel Thomas	Pte	21136	Wantage	Heilly Station Cemetery
24/08/1916	Pitt, Vio Douglas Wallace	2/Lieut			Warloy Baillon Comm Cem Ext
17/01/1916	Povey, John	Pte	18599	Pingewood	Chocques Mil Cem
02/07/1916	Priest, John Douglas	Pte	20005	Boreridge	Loos Brit Cem
26/09/1916	Prior, Edward James Farlow	Pte	36692	Lockinge	Millencourt Comm Cem Ext
25/07/1916	Pybus, Thomas	Pte	19043	Blackpool	Warloy Baillon Comm Cem Ext
15/04/1916	Rant, Thomas	Pte	13406	Hackney	Le Tréport Mil Cem
03/12/1916	Richards, William	Pte	37136	Willenhall	Warlencourt Brit Cem
23/04/1916	Robinson, Barrysdale Albert	Pte	17954	Henley on Thames	Bully-Grenay Comm Cem Fr Ext
06/09/1916	Rogers, George	Cpl	6528	Bearwood	St Sever Cem
25/09/1916	Rundle, William John	Pte	36694	Plymouth	Dernancourt Comm Cem Ext
01/06/1916	Rushen, Charles	Pte	13273	East Ham	Noeux-les-Mines Comm Cem
07/09/1916	Saunders, Edmund Arthur	Pte	21805	Baughurst	Flatiron Copse Cemetery
04/02/1916	Say, Charles Robert	Pte	17537	Southwark	Calais Southern Cem
01/06/1916	Smith, Charles Edward	Pte	14848	Streatley	Bully-Grenay Comm Cem
17/05/1916	Smith, Frederick George	L/Sgt	14033	Fulham	Chingford Mount Cemetery
04/03/1916	Smith, Harry	Pte	16287	Headington	Lapugnoy Mil Cem
03/06/1916	Smith, Sidney George	Pte	19001	Farnborough	Béthune Town Cem
25/09/1916	Stevenson, Jeremiah	Cpl	18801	Paddington	Dernancourt Comm Cem Ext
27/09/1916	Tarrant, Alfred	Pte	18021	Portsmouth	Dernancourt Comm Cem Ext
01/04/1916	Turner, Edwin	Pte	17687	Coventry	Le Tréport Mil Cem
24/03/1916	Upton, Percy	L/Cpl	18663	Holloway	Lillers Comm Cem
01/06/1916	Walker, William Henry	Pte	14912	Birmingham	Noeux-les-Mines Comm Cem
05/12/1916	Warburton, Kenneth	Pte	37150	Tilston	Dernancourt Comm Cem Ext
28/09/1916	Wilkins, Edward	Pte	18666	Brize Norton	St Sever Cem
24/08/1916	Wilkins, William	Pte	18805	Clewer	Flatiron Copse Cemetery

Appendix IV
Honours and awards for the 5th, 6th and 8th Battalions of the Royal Berkshire Regiment as announced in the London Gazette in 1916 (The date of announcement is given in brackets.)

5th Battalion

Military Cross

Capt George Galen Bartholomew RAMC attached (26-9-1916)
2/Lt Alfred David Breach (25-8-1916)
2/Lt Harold Masters Brown (25-8-1916)
Lt James Sidney Alexander Burton (26-9-1916)
Lt Lionel Dennis Cotterill (March 1916)
2/Lt Francis Andrew Lloyd Edwards (26-9-1916)
CSM 6859 Thomas Alfred Perkins (26-9-1916)
Capt Donat Ernest Ward (14-11-1916)
2/Lt Malcolm Wykes (26-9-1916)

Distinguished Conduct Medal

Pte 17231 S J Breathwick (20-10-1916)
Sgt 10431 Joseph Faulkner (20-10-1916)
Cpl 9099 R J Gee (15-3-1916)
Pte 10977 Fred Holford (11-3-1916)
Cpl 8000 Charles Percy Howard (22-9-1916)
Pte 10299 Albert Mansell (14-1-1916 & 11-3-1916)
Sgt 10375 Harry George Nicholls (22-9-1916)
Cpl 10633 Frank Powell (14-1-1916 & 11-3-1916)
CSM 10573 Alfred Waite (20-10-1916)
Pte 12810 E T B Ward (20-10-1916)

Military Medal

Pte 10283 Frederick James Allen (12-10-1916)
Pte 11117 Percy Alston (22-6-1916)
L/Cpl 10363 Frederick Amor (21-10-1916)
L/Cpl 12736 V Backman (21-10-1916)
Pte 10851 Thomas George Baker (21-10-1916)
L/Cpl 10660 George Bennett (21-10-1916)
Sgt 9499 J Bunce (23-8-1916)
Pte 11020 Alfred Clarke (21-10-1916)
Pte 10489 W Cousins (14-9-1916)
L/Cpl 9376 Albert Cox (9-12-1916)
Pte 8730 A W H Dobble (21-10-1916)
L/Cpl 9309 Grigg Francis Epsley (21-10-1916)
L/Sgt 6101 Walter Francis (21-10-1916)
Pte 9284 John Gardener (23-8-1916)
Pte 10441 J Garlick (14-9-1916)
L/Cpl 10502 Henry C Goddard (14-9-1916)
Sgt 8348 J Hackett (9-12-1916)
Cpl 7493 Walter Sidney Hammond (22-8-1916)
L/Cpl 9872 E Harwood (November 1916)
Cpl 19606 William H Hestor (21-10-1916)
L/Cpl 10563 Arthur Histead (14-9-1916)
Sgt 200795 J W Lambourne (19-9-1916)
Pte 11445 R H Langley (1-9-1916)
Pte 11197 Benjamin Thomas Livett (3-6-1916)
Pte 12016 James MacFarlane (22-8-1916)
Cpl 10506 Herbert John Matthews (21-10-1916)
Pte 10555 W Parris (21-10-1916)
L/Cpl 11375 William Vincent Henry Pearmine (23-8-1916)
Pte 10286 (35533) Lawrence William Perris (14-9-1916)

Pte 11763 F Pike (21-10-1916)
Pte 10254 Arthur James Purchell (23-8-1916)
L/Sgt 10861 James Redford (14-9-1916)
Cpl 15239 P Reynolds (14-9-1916)
Pte 15996 E Robbins (23-8-1916)
L/Cpl 18313 A J Scrivens (11-11-1916)
Pte 11129 Arthur Lloyd Smith (23-8-1916)
Sgt 10446 R H Tucker (14-9-1916)
Pte 7401 Charles W Webb (21-10-1916)
Sgt 10291 Edward Woodley (23-8-1916)

Bar to Military Medal

Pte 10441 J Garlick MM (21-10-1916)

Mentioned in Dispatches

Major D H Avory (16-6-1916)
Capt Oliver N Chadwyck-Healey (15-6-1916)
Lt Cecil Argo Gold (15-6-1916)
L/Cpl 10563 Arthur Histead (1-1-1916)
Sgt 14241 Benjamin L Nicholls (15-6-1916)
Pte 10555 L W Perris (1-1-1916)
2/Lt Roger Thomas Pollard (1-1-1916)
Cpl 15239 P Reynolds (15-6-1916)
CSM 9866 William Rixon (15-6-1916)
Capt Humphrey Stewart (15-6-1916)
Lt F Tuttle (15-6-1916)

Meritorious Service Medal

Sgt 9941 J Boyd (17-10-1916)

6th Battalion

Military Cross

Capt Harold Ackroyd RAMC attached (20-10-1916)
Lt Guy Saxon Llewellyn Gregson-Ellis (3-6-1916)
Capt Walter Phillip Hewetson (3-6-1916)
2/Lt Arthur Henry Tudor Lewis (11-12-1916)
2/Lt John Noel Richardson (20-10-1916)

Distinguished Conduct Medal

CSM 10298 Henry James Bartholomew (20-10-1916)
Sgt 10141 Tom Bowley (14-1-1916 & 11-3-1916)
Cpl 16491 W Moore (14-1-1916 & 11-3-1916)
Sgt R Ruffell (25-11-1916)
CSM 8244 F A Sayer (20-10-1916)
Sgt 12900 George Thomas Stanners (14-1-1916 & 11-3-1916)

Military Medal

L/Cpl 12512 W Angel (21-12-1916)
Sgt Tom Bowley (21-12-1916)
Pte 12726 Alfred James Caunt (21-12-1916)
Sgt 12631 T F Davis (11-11-1916)
L/Cpl 15638 William George Dewe (14-9-1916)
Pte 19320 S W Dobbinson (21-12-1916)

L/Cpl 12895 **Arthur George Edwards** (21-12-1916)
Pte 12975 **S Fenner** (21-10-1916)
L/Sgt 12872 **Frank Giddings** (21-10-1916)
Cpl 12656 **Frank Gough** (21-12-1916)
Pte 12887 **E Gray** (10-8-1916)
Pte 12047 **Joseph Harrison** (21-10-1916)
L/Cpl 12338 **Frederick Hodgetts** (21-10-1916)
L/Sgt 12512 **C Horwood** (21-12-1916)
Sgt 3016 **John William Lambourne** (21-9-1916)
Pte 200767 **Rowland G Ludlow** (11-11-1916)
L/Cpl 17196 **John Robert Mays** (11-11-1916)
Pte 15359 **Frederick Mickle** (21-12-1916)
L/Cpl 15379 **Ernest Pimm** (21-10-1916)
Pte 12492 **A Pritchett** (21-12-1916)
Pte 12321 **T Redfern** (11-11-1916)
Pte 24254 **H R Spencer** (21-12-1916)
Pte 17654 **W L Sullivan** (11-11-1916)
Cpl 12590 **James Taylor** (21-10-1916)
Pte 7401 **Charles W Webb** (21-10-1916)

Mentioned in Dispatches
2/Lt **Godfrey Mitchell Courage** (15-6-1916)
Lt-Col **A J W Dowell** (1-1-1916)
Capt **W P Hewetson** (1-1-1916)
Sgt 10365 **Frederick Everett Hurn** (15-6-1916)
Sgt 12487 **George Herbert Thomas** (1-1-1916)
Sgt 12417 **H J White** (15-6-1916)

8th Battalion

Military Cross
Capt **Cecil Steadman Cloake** (20-10-1916)
Lt **David J Footman** (June 1916)
2/Lt **Walter Cond Hanney** (25-8-1916)
Capt **J H G Lawrence** (New Years Honours List 1917)
2/Lt **Gordon Fraser Marsh** (New Years Honours List 1917)
Capt **Thomas Gerald Robinson** (New Years Honours List 1917)

Distinguished Conduct Medal
L/Sgt 16519 **Elias Evans** (30-3-1916)
Cpl 10686 **Charles Hayward** (21-6-1916)
Pte 18993 **G Mansfield** (22-9-1916)
Sgt 15574 **Henry John Musto** (21-6-1916)
Sgt 11246 **C A Oliver** (22-9-1916)
Cpl 16116 **Stephen J Smith** (24-6-1916)
Pte 18567 **G W Yates** (21-10-1916)

Military Medal
Cpl 16357 **A Andrews** (1-9-1916)
Sgt 18749 **S G Andrews** (1-9-1916)
Pte 14507 **Walter Arter** (9-12-1916)
Pte 14328 **William Arthur Ayres** (September 1916)
Pte 10913 **Fred Bailey** (14-11-1916)
Cpl 17958 **F Belcher** (1-9-1916)
Sgt 14349 **Jack Brown** (14-9-1916)
Pte 14627 **Herbert Cale** (14-9-1916)
Pte 14572 **David William Charley** (August 1916)
Pte 9615 **C Collins** (21-10-1916)
Pte 14494 **John Donovan** (9-12-1916)
L/Cpl 13098 **Percy Charles Double** (14-9-1916)

Pte 12197 **E Edwards** (10-8-1916)
Pte 14150 **Wallace Arthur Eldridge** (9-12-1916)
Pte 15255 **Albert William Eley** (14-9-1916)
Pte 15429 **John England** (14-9-1916)
Pte 12955 **P Fitt** (14-9-1916)
L/Sgt 14506 **A Fullbrook** (9-12-1916)
Pte 18140 (18491) **A H Gosling** (9-12-1916)
Pte 13570 **Edward Lynn Hall** (14-9-1916)
Sgt 39376 **E Hammond** (9-12-1916)
Pte 13067 **Reginald Hine** (14-9-1916)
Cpl 17311 **P Holmes** (10-8-1916)
L/Cpl 15609 **Edward Hughes** (9-12-1916)
Pte 13486 **L H May** (1-9-1916)
Pte 14582 **J A Petch** (14-9-1916)
Pte 18835 **Edward Poynter** (9-12-1916)
Pte 18434 **A J Rowe** (9-12-1916)
L/Cpl 15625 **George Charles Rowland** (10-8-1916)
L/Cpl 16362 **C Ruff** (10-8-1916)
Pte 10518 **R Slyfield** (1-9-1916)
Sgt 13229 **Henry John Turner** (3-6-1916)
Sgt 14851 **John James Woodfield** (3-6-1916)
L/Cpl 17842 **Walter Woodley** (22-10-1916)
L/Cpl 14954 **Thomas Wort** (14-9-1916)
Pte 18567 **G W Yates** (14-9-1916)

Mentioned in Dispatches
Lt-Col **C F N Bartlett** (New Years Honours List 1917)
Acting RSM 10001 **Cecil Brown** (15-6-1916)
Sgt 14349 **Jack Brown** (15-6-1916)
Pte 14572 **David William Charley** (15-6-1916)
L/Cpl 15638 **William George Dewe** (15-6-1916)
2/Lt **Thomas Bernard Lawrence** (1-1-1916)
Acting Sgt 12720 **John Ernest Moth** (15-6-1916)
Sgt 15220 **B Palmer** (15-6-1916)
Pte 14582 **J A Petch** (15-6-1916)
L/Cpl **Albert Alick Pounds** (15-6-1916)
L/Cpl 14950 **T H A Smart** (New Years Honours List 1917)
Capt **Douglas Tosetti** (1-1-1916)
CSM 13579 **William Edward Basil Woodhouse** (15-6-1916)

N.B. The London Gazette indicates only the regiments, not the battalions, in which the men were serving when the honour or award was approved. Some of the above who served in more than one battalion of the Royal Berkshire Regiment may have been serving in a different battalion at the time of the award. Others may have been omitted.

For gootness sake Halt !
der Royal Berks.
are koming.